1982

WHAT YOU SHOULD KNOW
BEFORE
YOU HAVE YOUR CAR REPAIRED

*By Anthony Till*_____

WHAT YOU SHOULD KNOW BEFORE YOU BUY A CAR

WHAT YOU SHOULD KNOW BEFORE YOU HAVE YOUR CAR
REPAIRED

WHAT YOU SHOULD KNOW BEFORE YOU HAVE YOUR CAR REPAIRED

Anthony Till

A SHERBOURNE PRESS HANDBOOK

SHERBOURNE PRESS, INC.   LOS ANGELES

Rights & Permissions Dept.
Sherbourne Press, Inc.
1640 So. La Cienega Blvd.
Los Angeles, Ca. 90035
Library of Congress Catalog Card Number 71-124334
ISBN—0-8202-0153-7
Second Printing

Manufactured in the United States of America by Kingsport Press, Inc., Kingsport, Tennessee

CONTENTS

	Introduction	7
1	What You Should Know About Automobile Mechanics	11
2	The Six Types of Automobile Repair Garages	18
3	Service and Repair Departments at New Car Dealerships	24
4	Those Franchised Muffler, Brake, and Transmission Shops	38
5	The Large Independent Garage	43
6	The Small One- or Two-Man Garage	49
7	Car Repairs at Gas Stations	58
8	Diagnostic Analysis Centers	65
9	Prevention Is Better Than Cure	88
10	How Good Is Your 5-Year-50,000 Mile New Car Warranty?	102
11	Accidents, Body Repairs, and Insurance Claims	121
	Appendix: Your Own Flat Rate Book	131
	Glossary of Terms	151

INTRODUCTION

This book is for every driver who has ever experienced that feeling of helplessness when the car decided to be stubborn, those unforgettable days when it refused to purr along in its usual happy style, or—even worse—when it decided to take the day off altogether and just stand there. Is there anything more agonizing than the struggle to raise the hood and then the realization that you know nothing at all about the intricacies before you?

Most people capitulate and make the inevitable telephone call to their local friendly garage, betraying both their ignorance and their vulnerability with the words, "Something seems to be wrong with my car."

This confession of mechanical unenlightenment offers to an unscrupulous service "advisor" a whole world of potential profit and high commissions. He might even ask a couple of slightly technical questions, just to be sure that he is dealing with what is known in the business as a "laydown," and then, having "qualified" the prospect, he will dispatch a tow truck to drag the patient into the garage. From that moment on, the uninformed motorist is completely and unutterably lost. His innocence is afforded no protection at all by the almost nonexistent statutes presently governing automobile mechanics and the automobile repair trade in general. There is nothing to discourage these get-rich-quick artists from padding the costs of minor and inexpensive adjustments. Just as a man dying of thirst would pay any price for water, it would seem that in this jungle we call civilization survival depends upon dependable transportation. Any price can be demanded, and obtained, from those who would keep up with the rest.

Perhaps you are one of the millions who have long had their suspicions about the car repair business, but insufficient know-how to recognize when they are being cheated. The following pages will give many examples that are par for the course at far too many of this nation's automobile service and repair shops. I've spent the past 25 years as part and parcel of the car business, and I washed the grease off my hands before sitting down at my typewriter to try to expose my chosen profession. You are going to be given a guided tour *behind the scenes* at the five basic types of automobile repair facilities, a full explanation of their methods of operation, and, for the first time, a startling introduction to some of the characters who operate them.

You will be told how to separate the good guys from the bad guys. Throughout this book, you will be given many tips which will enable you to correct for yourself many of the minor problems your car will encounter, which, until now, have always meant lost time at work and an expensive bill from the garage. This information alone should ensure that your comparatively small investment in the book will produce an excellent return. Technical or trade terms will not be used, as it is my intention that my words and advice be understood clearly by even the most delightfully helpless female. We'll leave valve jobs, brake relines, and transmission overhauls to the repair shops.

Most of the frustration suffered by today's motorists is caused by extremely minor and easily corrected problems. Let's see if we can't save you some time, money, and nervous tension by showing you how to try one or two simple corrective measures the very next time you have car troubles. This kind of information, as close as the bookshelf, must be preferable to always having to make that call for help no matter how easily correctable the car's problem is.

Just as I did in my first book, *What You Should Know Before You Buy a Car*, I'm taking verbal swipes only at those who would spoil a fine and essential service business. Those well-run establishments that earnestly try to serve the public well and charge a fair price for their skills can only gain in stature and patronage by an examination such as this. It might be a good idea if my readers took a long, hard look at those garage owners, service managers, and mechanics who protest too strongly when confronted with these charges, just as, on the other hand, you might do worse than to find a reason to patronize those garages and mechanics who manifest their delight at such revelations by applauding these and similar endeavors.

1

WHAT YOU SHOULD KNOW ABOUT AUTOMOBILE MECHANICS

There are very few trades or professions that do not insist that their members be licensed by a governing body. How many of us would continue to patronize our wonderful airlines if we were not confident that those jet engines and that vital equipment had been diligently checked out by highly skilled engineers, men who had studied long and well before passing the most stringent trade examinations, thus earning the right to display with pride the Federal Aviation Administration certificates testifying to their proficiency?

Even your barber must display an approved trade diploma which guarantees to each potential customer that he is indeed skilled and has passed the examinations set according to the standards of his trade. Thus, we can enter a barber shop even in a strange city and confidently expect to emerge with our hair skillfully cut by a qualified artisan.

Almost every trade or profession is headed by a select body of men whose main purpose is to set and maintain minimum standards of skills and ethics. Where the public safety is involved, either state or federal authorities usually insist on involving themselves, and thus the system of checks and balances is allowed to prevail.

There is, however, one enormous group of tradesmen who appear to have been granted some kind of diplomatic immunity—an entire profession whose skills and attitudes decide whether or not each one of us lives or dies every day! How many people in this nation of more than 200 million can claim that, for one single day, they were completely independent of the skills of the auto mechanic? Even those who do not venture onto the highways will almost certainly have to walk across a street in front of cars and trucks that may or may not be able to stop in time. How can any investigator approach a pile of twisted and burned junk that was once a beautiful automobile and decide that its destruction was caused by inferior driving, rather than by the simple fact that the car had been worked on by some incompetent fool who did not really know the difference between a strut rod and a tie rod? If some unfortunate barber with a hangover takes a little too much off the top, you can express your contempt for his abilities and avoid his establishment from that day forth. The incompetent mechanic is never subjected to this indignity, as most of his mistakes are buried six feet under the ground.

Automobile mechanics are not tested in this country. Automobile mechanics do not serve five years of indentured apprenticeship in this country, as they must do throughout most of the civilized world. Automobile mechanics in this country are not controlled by any trade organization, or by any state or federal government agency. In other words, anyone can become an automobile mechanic tomorrow, simply by calling himself one and by persuading some overworked and understaffed garage owner to employ him.

Get this straight now, automobile mechanics in the United States have no set standards of skill. A man can be washing dishes today and adjusting your steering gear tomorrow. In almost every other country in the world, and this includes many of the most backward and undeveloped areas, no man is permitted to sell his services as an automobile mechanic unless he has in his possession either an A, a B, or a C certificate issued by the automobile trade governing body. This denotes his abilities and standard of skill, and indicates to any potential employer the type of repair that he can be entrusted with. Here, in this great country, it would seem that more importance is attached to the skills of your barber than to the ability of the man who repairs your car.

"Factory trained mechanics" is an intentionally misleading term used by almost every new car dealership in the land on display signs and advertising. What it really means is that a couple of the mechanics have attended a one- or two-day seminar in order that a factory technician can explain to them how to install some new gadget or how to overcome some mechanical weakness which should never have been permitted to find its way into the design of the car in the first place. It's a system which works in the long run, however. Today's mechanics learn from their mistakes. Most of them are bright enough not to make the same mistakes repeatedly. One day a guy does something wrong, the next day he does a better job, and the day after an even better result is obtained. The system is called, I believe, "on the job training." Undoubtedly it contributes to the prosperity of doctors, hospitals, morticians, tow truck operators, body repair shops, and freeway divider repair men. Unfortunately for us all, the sign on the dealership is just another deception. The automobile manufacturers do not train mechanics for their franchised dealerships. They do not discourage their dealerships from making this kind of misleading statement, either.

All you need to know about defending yourself against consumer fraud as it is practiced at many service and repair garages is contained in these pages. All you need to do is to study it and absorb it carefully in order to save yourself many, many hundreds of dollars in the years to come.

Lesson number one you have just completed. Automobile mechanics in this country *do not repair cars. They do not know how.* All they do is install new parts. Almost every repair order nowadays reads, "Remove and replace . . ." Rarely, if ever, will you find a repair order which begins, "Remove and *repair* . . ." A mechanic's pride in his work and skills has been almost eliminated by the introduction of the manufacturer's *Flat Rate Book* (much more about this later), which prices the work of the skilled on the same level as the unskilled and which certainly discourages the careful diligence of the old-time craftsman, whose pride would insist that he check and recheck his work before permitting his customer to drive the car out on the roads again. Nowadays, most of the road testing after a repair is done by the customer himself after he picks the car up, in order that the mechanic can hurry on to the next job. This state of affairs not only results in terrible accidents, but also is the reason why so many irate customers bring their cars back to the garage for further adjustments. Customers should insist that, before they pay their repair bill and drive away, one of the service department managers accompany them on a short test drive so that they can satisfy themselves that the repairs they are being asked to pay for have been completed to their satisfaction.

Ideally, we should adopt a recruiting and training system similar to that of the European countries. They take young men straight from school as apprentices. As a rule, these youngsters either have failed to qualify for college or prefer to start working as soon as their high school education is completed. They are sent to technical colleges and trade schools for two whole days every week and spend the rest of their time working under the strict supervision of an experi-

enced A-licensed automotive engineer. They are profession-
ally trained to become all-around experts in every type of
repair on every type of automobile. Thus, when their training
is completed and their trade examinations have been passed,
they are reliable craftsmen instead of inept bunglers. During
their education, European apprentices are taught how to use
lathes, grinders, drilling machines, and everything that will
help them throughout their careers, so that it is not an unusual sight to find them later actually in the garage's machine
shop making parts and devices which will improve the performance of customers' automobiles.

In sad comparison to Europe, we have no standards of
engineering excellence in our repair garages. The situation is
frightening and should not be tolerated. This great country
has more automobiles on its streets than any other country
in the world. We have more beautiful highways, more repair
garages, more committees to improve highway safety, and
more student driver training facilities. Sadly, we also have
more deaths and injuries on our highways, more insurance
claims, more smog resulting mainly from poorly tuned and
serviced automobiles, and certainly the highest-paid automobile mechanics. Our serious smog situation would be cut
by more than 50 percent if the skills of our tune-up mechanics
could be improved by 20 percent!

Ask yourself how the authorities can reconcile this situation with the fact that before you and I can drive a car on the
public streets, we must pass a test of driving skill. Quite properly, society is entitled to know that we are not going to
endanger other drivers or pedestrians. Yet, if we decide to do
a little moonlighting, as many do, by taking a spare-time job
in a garage installing brake linings, no test of our skill is required or even available. So we have a set of circumstances
which must inevitably lead to disaster and carnage: an automobile which weighs about two tons, a competent driver
with a license to prove his driving skills, travelling along a

beautiful highway with perfect road markings and warning signals. At 65 miles an hour, our competent driver on our beautiful and well-marked highway finds himself approaching an intersection or a line of halted vehicles. In plenty of time he depresses his brake pedal—and finds that he has no brakes. . . When the mortuary wagon and the ambulances have left the scene, and the mangled steel has been pushed to the side of the road, it is likely that someone will remark, "I saw the whole thing, that idiot never even tried to stop. He must have been drunk, or sick." How many of us would wonder about the guy who installed those brakes? Why would we? After all, aren't all automobile mechanics "factory trained?"

If legislation could be enacted over the powerful protests of the automobile and oil company lobbies to bring our standards of required mechanical skills to a par with those of most other nations throughout the world, it is my belief that not one currently employed automobile mechanic in ten could pass the tests which must now be passed by mechanics in the European countries. To further dramatize the seriousness of the situation which we have allowed ourselves to get into, if a law was passed today which required that such tests be taken before an automobile mechanic could be licensed and permitted to work on our cars, millions of cars which now splutter and cough their way across our nation would slowly but surely come to a grinding halt. In many instances, it is only our hit-or-miss, unskilled or semi-skilled parts replacers that keep them running.

I know of no statutes, either state or federal, that govern automobile repairs. I know of no laws that protect us from the automobile industry's repair business. Here's the kicker, friends: there aren't going to be any, either. Auto mechanics are not going to be tested to prove their professional status. If they are ever licensed by the state in which they are employed, it will simply mean that the state legislature has found another method of producing taxes, by charging every automobile mechanic perhaps $10 a year for a license. The day when automobile mechanics must pass a strict trade examination will come when the automobile and oil company lobbies have been kicked out of the dark corners of our halls of government, so please don't hold your breath. . .

Automobile mechanics are not licensed or tested in this country. Now that we know this, perhaps we can learn how to be a lot more discriminating in our choice of repair facilities. This one piece of information alone will surely result in at least one little group, my readers, saving not only a considerable amount of money over the years, but also the anguish and frustration of unsatisfactory repair work and of having to go back to the garage to complain to an unsympathetic service salesman again and again. It is also more than possible that an even more vital saving might result: our very lives.

2

THE SIX TYPES OF AUTOMOBILE REPAIR GARAGES

Today's motorists seem to classify all auto repair businesses under the same general heading. Oh, they have an idea that some are larger and better equipped than others, and that the large and seemingly well-equipped establishment will do a better job, even though it will probably cost a little more. After all, there is something very reassuring about those white-coated mechanical "doctors" who listen to our usually half-baked attempts to explain our needs and then proceed to insist that we sign a repair order, giving them a mechanic's lien on our car until we pay for whatever repairs and replacements they decide to make.

Before we get too deeply involved in exposing the vampires of the automobile repair business, and in order to clear away some of the fog that has for too long shrouded the modus operandi of many of its operators, let me first list the six different types of repair facilities now available in almost every city and town across the United States and Canada.

Every auto repair garage comes under one of the six following headings: (1) New car dealerships with attached service and parts departments. (2) The large independent general repair garages with at least a dozen service stalls and no less than six hoists. (3) Garages franchised by national companies and supported by very heavy advertising, which specialize in selling and installing the parent company's rebuilt engines, transmissions, brakes, or mufflers. (4) The small one- or two-man garage with premises in the low-rent part of town, where the proprietor usually crawls out from under a car to greet you. (5) The many thousands of gas stations with their one or two service stalls. These clearly outnumber every other kind of repair facility and are responsible for most of the minor repairs and adjustments made on today's automobiles. (6) A comparative newcomer in this market, the automobile analysis or diagnostic centers, which undertake to give any car a complete electronic test and to report any faults the car may have for a fee. Almost without exception, these are franchised operations and are individually owned by gentlemen whose standards of ethics can, with fairness, be described as varying.

In this introductory chapter, we will just take a step or two inside the entrance at each of these six types of repair shops. At this stage, we won't get into any of the larcenies and nefarious practices indulged in by many of them. You will just be shown around and told what your money will buy at these different operations, some of the advantages that one type of shop has over another, and some of the limitations of all six.

We will start at the typical new car dealership's service department. At this type of establishment, the public naturally expects cars to be serviced by highly skilled factory trained artisans, using only the very latest tools, equipment, and genuine factory replacement parts. Customers here can be categorized under two headings: those taking advantage of the terms of their new car factory warranty, and those motorists who are prepared to pay a little more for what they expect to be the best service available for their particular brand of automobile.

Except where such a dealership maintains a dishonest attitude toward its customers, there can be little doubt that a car owner with mechanical problems will have them cured and will soon have his automobile back on the job. For reasons which will be explained in the chapter on this type of service department, however, while curing the patient's asthmatic condition, the doctor may throw in and charge for healing a sprained ankle and a stiff neck, neither of which was interfering with the car's satisfactory performance.

A quick look now at the large independent garage with no franchise attachments to either a new car manufacturer or a muffler or transmission manufacturer. In almost every case, this operation is the result of healthy growth from a one-man workshop or of successful management of a dealership service department, and it competes with the dealerships in offering good, dependable work and reasonable prices. I find that at most of these large independents, good old-fashioned American business enterprise can still be seen working, without any dependence on gimmick offers or a reputation purchased for a fee from the franchise houses. One gets the impression that here a small businessman did good work and gave good value to a few, who recommended him to a few more, and so on until he was able to enlarge his premises and take on more mechanics to handle the demand for his standards of skill and value. For as long as he maintains these attributes, his business will grow.

If you are fortunate enough to patronize one of these gentlemen who is on his way up, especially one who is recommended by a recent customer, there is little doubt that you will obtain reliable repairs at a fair price. Indeed, you should look no further whenever your car is in need of repairs.

Let us now visit any of the nationally franchised garages,

which seem to be springing up almost as thickly as the multitudinous franchise hamburger stands. Here, the parent company's product is sold and installed exclusively: usually either mufflers, brakes, rebuilt transmissions, or engines. It has always seemed to me that the motoring public is misled by this type of operation. An unending flow of television and radio commercials and newspaper advertising induces most people to believe that this is one large company with hundreds of branches or service centers throughout the country. The truth is, of course, that each of these garages is individually owned and operated by a businessman who pays for the use of a nationally advertised name and an identity with the parent company's signs, trade-marks, and modus operandi. Determining the amount and quality of service given to customers is still the prerogative of each operator. There will be much to tell about this type of repair service in a later chapter.

Under our fourth heading we find the small, one-man back street repair shop. No flashy signs here, of course, and the garage is usually kept so busy that the owner will tell you that there never seems to be enough time to give the place a good cleaning. If the rent is low and the proprietor is skilled and industrious, this can be quite a good business once a reputation has been established among the local community. However, there are some serious impediments to high-quality workmanship involved here, and these, together with the obvious lower cost advantages for the clients, will be fully developed in the pages to follow.

We will certainly not have to travel very far to find the next type of repair service on our list. Gas stations are just about everywhere, and most of them could hardly stay in business were it not for the extra income they derive from car repairs and service. Collectively, they must be responsible for more than half of the minor repairs, oil changes, and lubrications given to the country's automobiles. It is my view that many of these conveniently located service stations are of great value to the motoring public. Woe betide us all when our cars develop problems at night or on weekends, were it not for the seemingly ever-open gas stations. One word of warning, however: the skills available at the gas stations will run the entire gamut of quality, ranging from the very worst to the very best, and certainly some knowledge of the available mechanic's background and training should be obtained before entrusting your valuable automobile to his tender mercies and what may well be his trial-and-error skills.

The sixth and last type of repair facility that we are going to examine is such a new innovation that it's possible some readers will learn about it here for the first time. It will call itself either an "automobile diagnostic center" or an "automobile analysis center." The advertising will catch your attention by offering to give your car a "complete diagnostic analysis" for something like $12.95 (for a four-cylinder car). Sound good? I guess most of us would like to know how healthy our cars are every now and again, and this sounds like a lot for such a small fee, right? Sorry folks. In spite of what the man on the commercial said, this is just another auto repair shop using a new twist to attract business. Much more about this one later on.

There you have them, the six varieties of automobile repair business, and they can all be found within a few blocks, no matter where you live in this country. Which is best for you? All of them have a service to offer . . . and almost all of them will be trying to get their hands in your pockets.

At this time, there seems to be no way that the dishonest repair shops can be eliminated altogether. It's going to take a lot more than the customary indulgent attitude on the part of our legislators to correct the outrageous situation which allows untrained, unskilled, and unlicensed mechanics to fumble their way through our car repairs. Try to recall the last time you read in your newspaper that a dealership or a repair shop was convicted of fraud or anything else. If you can recall a case which went against them, I would surely like to read of it. So I want my readers to be realistic and acknowledge at least to themselves that those dealers and garage owners who, by their plans of compensation for their employees, have been responsible for defrauding the motoring public for so many years are not exactly filling our jails at this time, nor are they ever likely to be. You must therefore learn how to protect yourselves by letting them see that you have taken your course in automotive self-defense. Here is such a course. Just as with a course in boxing or karate, you are not going to win all of your early bouts, but if you manage to retain only half of the information and defensive strategies they're going to know they've been in a fight. Once they understand that you are one little guy who might hurt them, they will do what all bullies would do in a similar situation: treat you with a great deal of respect and give you a fair shake when it comes to repairing your car.

Study the following pages carefully, and their contents will serve you well the next time some automotive bandit in a white coat starts to take advantage of you and your immobilized automobile.

3

SERVICE AND REPAIR DEPARTMENTS AT NEW CAR DEALERSHIPS

There are only two kinds of new car dealerships, honest ones and dishonest ones. Anything in between these two standards can only be described, in my opinion, as a dishonest establishment. It will be interesting to see how many dealerships will shriek their protests that my blanket condemnation is too strong; that they do not do this or that, and that I am being grossly unfair to those who only practice one or two of the larcenies that I am about to describe. With great sanctimoniousness, they will protest wrathfully at being placed in the same category as common criminals. In other words, they will insist that they are, like the proverbial naive young lady, just a little bit pregnant. . . .

To those who will claim that they would be forced out of business if they did not abide by the ground rules laid down by their competitors, or that their tactics are an integral part of the good old American free enterprise system, I say "Baloney!" There is no greater devotee of the free enterprise system than myself, and if taking advantage of motorists with car troubles is a laudable part of that system, then it's high time something was done about it. There is nothing wrong with "horse-trading," or with one businessman outfoxing another, but there must be something sick about the toad who takes the pennies from a blind man's dish. There is even an admission of this kind of guilt in common usage in the car business. The phrase is, "It's just like taking candy from a baby." Is there really very much difference between the blind man, the baby, and the typical motorist who confesses to a *commission only* service salesman that there is something wrong with his or her car?

The examples of dishonesty to be given here are not examples of the way the automobile trade was operated in the old days. Almost without exception, these are the latest innovations, introduced during the past ten years or so. All of them are in common usage right now, so beware of the smooth operator who attempts to convince you that my charges stem from many years ago. The opposite is true, I'm afraid. This is borne out by a growing sound of protest from the motoring public as more and more of the old-style quality service dealerships capitulate and join the ranks of the automotive racketeers. I once spent a considerable time as general manager of a large and extremely successful new car dealership where the service repair department made astronomical profits. I did not dare to change the modus operandi of this department, and when I received the appointment it was with the clear understanding that I would do nothing that would place any checks or limits on this department's "golden goose." There was no great secret about its prosperity. The simple rule was that if a customer managed to get out of there without being screwed, then someone was falling down on the job. Here, the only employees who worked for a salary were the three girls who worked in the office, the parts truck driver, and the old guy who swept the yard and cleaned up. Everyone else, from the service manager on down, was on a share of the "take." The higher the customer's bill, the more money everyone made. There was just no way for a customer to escape with his car before he paid what almost amounted to a ransom.

The best place to start is always the beginning, so let us find out more about the first man you encounter when you drive into a new car dealership's service department. You will be approached by a man who will introduce himself as your "service advisor." In the trade he is known as a service writer or service salesman. In some dealerships they call themselves assistant service managers, but no matter what he calls himself, in reality he is plainly and simply a commissioned salesman, whose only aim is to sell you as many repairs and replacements as he can. His task is fairly simple, much easier than the new car salesman's. After all, it would not be easy for a new car salesman to sell you a very large red car if you had decided on a very small blue one, right? On the other hand, if you drive into the service department to have a muffler installed, it is not difficult to convince you that your brakes are unsafe, that your tie rods are loose, and that it's high time your engine was given a major tune-up. The average motorist is so uninformed and easily alarmed at the possibility of physical harm to himself or his family that it is rare indeed for one of them not to be impressed by the service salesman's grim foreboding.

The "sell or starve" type of pay plan under which almost all service advisors operate is responsible for much of the fraud that is perpetrated on the unenlightened motorist. A truthful service salesman who gave each customer an honest appraisal of his mechanical needs would never make a living wage, and would certainly not keep the job for very long. If he is to take home a good paycheck, he must either disregard any decent ethical standards he brought to the job with him or else take up a different line of work. His victims rarely offer any resistance because not one in a thousand has the least idea of what goes on under the hood of a car. They know that they desperately need the use of their car, and in order to regain its benefits they are prepared to agree to almost anything the service "advisor" *advises*.

Let's examine an all-too-frequent situation. Mom or Dad gets into the family car, turns on the ignition, and goes through the motions of getting it started. Like most people, they have at this stage exhausted their knowledge of automobile engineering, and so they are immediately alarmed when, on this particular morning, their usually dependable automobile refuses to produce its customary quiet hum, and that exhilarating surge of power is conspicuous by its absence. Instead, the car seems to shake and emit dreadful sounds. Pumping on the gas pedal results only in the engine quitting altogether, and the frenzied attempts to restart it only result in running the battery down altogether.

Typically, the man in this predicament will utter the customary expletives, get out of the car, and raise the hood. He will stare belligerently first at the air cleaner, then at the side of the engine block, and finally at the radiator. When this course of action produces nothing beneficial, he will more than likely walk around the front of the car and repeat the process from the other side. I have often wondered what is going on in people's minds while they go through this pretentious ceremony, and I can only assume that they must be quietly wishing that they knew something about the mechanics of their car, or that some automotive expert would just happen to come walking along the street at that time who would agree to help them out. After satisfying himself that all of the automotive experts in the world are somewhere else at that particular moment, our typical motorist will slide behind the wheel for one last despairing attempt to start the ailing engine. The battery is by now quite exhausted and expires with a sickening gasp or choking "clicks."

"What seems to be the trouble?" The service advisor's

query seems kindly and innocent enough when he picks up the telephone. In reality, he is asking, "Do you know anything about automobiles?"

If the customer's reply is, "I've got a cracked distributor cap, could you send someone round with a new one?" then he knows that he's not going to make much of a commission from this joker. On the other hand, when the caller responds, as almost all of them do, with something like, "I just can't get the darned thing to start this morning and I seem to have run my battery down," then his day begins to brighten considerably. He takes down the name and address and makes a mental note of the client's mechanical innocence before sending the tow truck out to bring the inert automobile and its somewhat bewildered owner to the garage.

Once there, the motorist is instructed to sign a repair order authorizing work to commence and agreeing to pay the tab in full before possession of the vehicle will be returned to him. The service salesman assures him that the car will be examined by an expert just as soon as one is free and that they will call him at his home or place of business with an estimate of the costs involved before they proceed with any major repairs. Most new car dealerships have loan cars available at from $5 to $10 a day, and once these papers have also been signed, the customer is sent on his way with the promise that he will be called on the telephone just as soon as the car has been checked out.

This is a situation which occurs several times a day at every new car dealership across the country. Let us call it act one. The curtain is raised on act two when the telephone rings either at the "unhorsed" victim's home or office, and he is informed that the car's fuel and ignition systems have been checked out and a new set of plugs and points has been installed; the car is now running again, but not very well. He is told that the mechanic is of the opinion that one of the pistons is broken and would like permission to pull the heads and take a look.

What can the poor customer do in a situation like this? He *must* have the use of his car, and he doesn't know enough even to question the service salesman about his problem. After a pregnant pause, during which he prepares himself for a financial setback, the unfortunate motorist almost always responds with, "How much is all of this going to cost?"

"Well, sir, so far there's the charge for the tow truck, that's $10. We've installed new points, plugs, and condenser and given the car a tune-up. Your timing was off quite a bit as well, so after resetting that, we have a total of $16.80 for parts and $28 for labor. With the $10 for the tow truck, that's $54.80 so far."

If this all has a familiar ring, it's because it has happened to you, probably more than once, in the past. It happens every year to the tune of more than $25 *billion* paid by motorists with car troubles to repair garages. This money is handed over almost entirely without question or investigation, either by the public or by any state or federal government agency.

In the case that we have just been describing, the unfortunate sucker would be lucky if he got his car back with a bill for less than $200. New car dealerships are the worst offenders at this type of fraud, mainly because of the way the manufacturers *advise* them to operate through the pay plans of the service manager, the service salesmen, and the mechanics, and the iniquitous *Flat Rate Book*.

"Now, sir, do you want us to go ahead and fix your car or would you like to come and pick it up the way it is?"

From bitter experience, most of you know what your response to this ultimatum must be. Without the use of your car in this society, you are like a bird without wings, a fish without water. . . Let's face it, you're a man without a job. You have no reason to believe that you are dealing with an aspiring Al Capone, so you probably shrug philosophically and say, "Go ahead and fix it. How soon can I pick up my car?"

You will never know if your trouble really was a cracked distributor cap, will you? A new cap costs about $2, and the labor time involved in changing the caps would be no more than a couple of minutes. Not much commission there for a service salesman, a mechanic, a service manager, and a dealership to share, is there?

There is, of course, no way that you can check out this possibility after you have agreed to have the work done that they suggested. Not for one moment would they consider trying to get away with just changing the distributor cap and then charging you for work which had not been done. They'll do all of the work they suggested, but instead of the miniscule profit they would have made from just the distributor cap, they will enjoy the very acceptable margin of a $200 repair bill.

How can you defend yourself against this kind of tyranny? Only, I'm afraid, by taking the time to learn about different types of automobile repair shops and by asking one or two informed questions.

Who's to blame for this ever-worsening situation? I would have to head my short list of culprits with the new car manufacturers, who devised and almost forcibly installed the incentive systems and the *Flat Rate Book* charges at every new car dealership in the U.S.A. As new car production lines became more and more automated, new cars began to spew out of the factories at an ever-increasing rate. Dealerships which for years had conducted very profitable and reputable businesses were sold a bill of goods by the manufacturers and cajoled into going "volume." "Don't sit around all day waiting for a buyer to give you $600 profit on a new car," they were told. "Sell three cars at $200 profit each, and you'll have the buyers lined up waiting to do business with you."

At first, only a few dealers sold out to the volume selling idea. They knew that there wouldn't be much margin left out of $200 to give each customer good after-sale service once the rest of the overhead had been deducted. Unfortunately, they eventually had to go along with the trend as they saw more and more of their old customers taking their business to the so-called discount houses. Things very quickly deteriorated, and it soon became apparent, even to the ruthless manufacturers, that if something was not done to help the new car dealers most of them would be forced out of business.

One thing the manufacturers were not prepared to do was reduce the output of their automated assembly lines. Instead, they produced a method of increasing the dealer's service and parts departments profits enough to compensate for their losses in new car sales. As dealers found themselves forced deeper and deeper into the price war which the manufacturers nurtured and encouraged with their enormous national advertising campaigns, more and more of the old-time standards of quality and service had to be discarded. The car-buying public was even advised by the manufacturers to "chisel" whenever they bought a new car. People became so brainwashed with this idea that I've seen families dragging around from dealership to dealership and travelling many miles looking for another $25 discount on the new model of their choice.

These same people are the first in line with demands for free service and adjustments after they finally buy a car, and instead of venting their anger on the real culprits, the greedy manufacturers who started the whole stinking mess, they scream their fury at some unfortunate dealership which they have forced to give away that last $50 which would otherwise have been gladly spent on giving them some decent after-sales service. New car dealerships would normally spend about $45 just on preparing a new car for delivery. In some areas, the price war has become so ridiculous that the place which "beats the deal" of its competitors is the one that just washes the new car and delivers it to the customer exactly the way it comes from the factory. Thus you have a customer who has made a "good deal," but who has a car that has not been checked out by a mechanic. A new car that has not been tightened and adjusted in all of the right places before delivery is destined to become very quickly what we in the business refer to as a "turkey." Just remember this the next time some sales manager offers you a deal that is $50 better than you could get from your own local dealership.

Perhaps I have succeeded in showing you that today, there is just no way for a new car dealership to make a satisfactory return on its investment in the new car sales department. Nationally, last year, the average profit per new car sold by all of the dealerships in the U.S. was slightly more than 2 percent, and this includes the fortunate ones that made as much as 5 percent per car, those who managed to just get by, and the many who were forced out of business altogether.

What has all of this got to do with the new car dealership's service and repair department? Plenty! It is the basic cause of almost all of the problems which now plague the unfortunate motorist whenever he requires service or repairs on that good buy he thought he'd made. It stands to reason that no businessman worth his salt is going to pay the salaries of a large office staff, plus the rent and overhead on that large, marble-pillared showroom, and carry a stock of new automobiles worth about a million dollars unless he can be shown how to make the whole thing worthwhile. Take a guess who showed him how to compensate for the situation in the new car showroom. You remember that 2 percent average profit we just mentioned? Now, you're probably asking yourself why he wouldn't just sell out and transfer his funds from his bank checking account to the same bank's savings department, where he'd get a 5 percent minimum annual return without work or risk, right?

"Don't do it!" the manufacturers screamed, "we'll show you what to do." *And they did.* Today, Americans spend $29 billion every year buying new cars, but they also spend $25 billion having their cars repaired. It's this $25 billion that helps to compensate the new car dealers for their problems up front in the new car showroom. Here, now, is an explanation of the system imposed by the manufacturers on all of their franchised new car dealerships. Follow this carefully and you'll be ahead of the game.

When a car is left at a new car dealership for service or repairs, the service salesman, or service advisor, as he will usually call himself, will move it to the service parking area, or, if his is full, he will park it outside in the street. Before locking it up, he will place a tag with a number in large figures either on the roof or inside the car on top of the dash. He will then take the keys and the service repair order, signed by the customer, to the service department office. The keys will then be tagged with the same number and hung on a large key board. Depending on the kind of service or repairs indicated on the repair order, it will be dropped into one of the slots of an enormous wall file under "Tune-ups," "Transmissions," "Brakes," "Front Ends," or the like.

In today's new car dealership service departments, each stall is equipped to specialize in certain tasks only. As indicated before, highly skilled automobile mechanics are extremely scarce, and so, as a general rule, these service stalls are manned by men who have received some training at one or two specific tasks. They perform these operations over and over, and thus some do become quite adept and speedy at their repetitious functions. Little or no repairing is ever done nowadays at new car dealerships, and with very few exceptions these so-called mechanics know only how to remove one part and replace it with a new one.

Certainly it would seem that a great deal of labor time is saved by this system, and your first reaction after learning about it might well be one of approval. You would quite understandably expect that whenever the time spent by a mechanic is shortened like this, your repair bill would be greatly reduced by the lower cost for the mechanic's time, right? Alas, friends, I must disillusion you all once again. Remember what I was telling you about the manufacturers compensating the dealers for their skinny profits in the new car sales department? Here it is, the secret weapon supplied to all new car dealerships by the new car manufacturers: the *Flat Rate Book*.

When you drive into any of this country's domestic new car dealership service departments, you drive out of the world of free enterprise and business competition and into the most rigidly controlled price-fixing racket in the world. No matter where you are in this country, the charge for labor will vary only by the going rate for labor in that area. The *number of hours* of labor that you will be charged for will always be the same. Thus, if you own a Chevrolet and you need your brakes relined, the number of hours of labor you will pay for will be the same, no matter which Chevrolet dealership does the job for you. At the time this is being written, every Chevrolet dealership in the United States will charge you for 2.1 hours of labor to replace the brake shoes on any Chevrolet, provided they are the standard drum brakes. Those Chevvys with disc brakes on the front will be charged for 1.8 hours of labor. Corvettes with disc brakes on all four wheels will be charged for just 1.1 hours. If you are the owner of any Chevrolet with the standard type of drum brakes, you're going to pay for more than two hours of labor, even if the job is completed by the mechanic in less than one hour. As most mechanics now are paid a share of the labor charged to the customer (usually 50 percent), all of the incentives are there to encourage hurried and inevitably careless work.

Every possible adjustment, replacement, and repair is indexed and given a time allowance in each manufacturer's *Flat Rate Book*. If you take a look at a couple of pages

chosen at random from the *Flat Rate Book* of a leading manufacturer used by all of their franchised dealerships, you will
note that each operation is allocated an exact amount of
time in hours. Thus, 1.6 hours is one hour and 36 minutes,
0.9 hours equals 54 minutes, and so on. If the charge for labor
at a particular dealership is $9.50 per hour, then a job which
is allocated a time allowance of one hour and 36 minutes by
the manufacturer's *Flat Rate Book* is going to cost the customer $15.20 for labor alone, even if the mechanic manages
to complete the task in 45 minutes.

The dealership profits under this "heads we win, tails you
lose" system, because during the course of one working day,
a fast mechanic might complete six or seven two-hour tasks
in eight hours, even though the manufacturer stipulates
that he should take almost 15 hours. So the mechanic has all
of the incentive he needs, especially if he is being paid 50
percent of the labor charges. Is it surprising that some mechanics earn as much as $75 for a single day's work? Not
really, when you realize that his customers have been coerced
into paying him for 15 hours work when in fact he has only
worked for eight hours.

There you have a good example of the manufacturers' "sell
new cars or get out" merchandising and the way the dealers
are compensated for it at the expense of the service department customers. Under this iniquitous system, the service
customer is usually charged for more labor time than was
put into the job. Any good automobile mechanic can beat
the *Flat Rate Book* times, and if anyone challenges my contention that it is stealing if a customer is charged for two
hours labor when the work was completed in one hour, then
my challenger must have an entirely different set of honesty
standards than this writer. The customer is always charged
according to the *Flat Rate Book*, and any short cuts that a
wily and experienced mechanic can take, and there are
plenty, just help to pad both his and his employer's income,

and allow the dealership to subsidize its new car sales department's efforts to compete in the fierce marketplace of new car sales.

At the end of this book you will find your very own *Flat Rate Book*. It has been compiled from all of the different manufacturers' books now in use, and it is complete in every detail. Every possible repair, replacement, and adjustment is included. Just call the service department of any new car dealership where you are considering having your car repaired or serviced and ask them how much they charge per hour for labor; then, with the help of this, your own flat rate book, you can figure out just how much your labor charges are going to be. Parts will always be charged out separately on your bill at full retail list price, and a call to the company's parts department will enable you to get these prices also, provided you know the parts that are going to be needed.

You will never find dealerships competing with each other on prices for repairs, and if that doesn't give you cause for incredulity, nothing ever will! You have all grown accustomed to the new car dealers' advertisements quoting discounted prices for their new cars. Have you ever seen any of these new car dealerships advertising their prices for repairs?

There you have the picture of what has happened to almost all new car dealerships since real salesmanship and quality customer service were sacrificed on the altar of discount and volume selling. With their new car sales profits trimmed down to a paltry $200 or $300 per car, dealerships can no longer tolerate any kind of loss in the service department such as was provided for in the old days. Free after-sales service may still be implied in some dealerships' advertising, but in reality it no longer exists at any of the volume-minded operations. Only the toughest and most hardnosed dealerships can survive in today's fiercely competitive market, and unfortunately for the new car customers, it is this tough, merciless demeanor which they must contend with—not only when they buy a new car, but also later when they bring their purchases into the service departments for adjustments and repairs.

There is another department in every new car dealership which, in most instances, will take advantage of the unfortunate owner of a sick automobile. This is the parts department. It is run quite independently as a separate business and usually pays its manager and countermen an important commission on the parts they sell. Keep in mind that the service department sells only the questionable skills of its mechanics and the use of its tools and equipment. All new parts installed by the mechanics are charged out at full retail price by the parts department insofar as the customer's bill is concerned. There is a discount given, but it is given to the service department as an encouragement for them to sell more and more parts to their captive and defenseless customers. Even when a car in for repair is sent out to another company to have items like air conditioning or tires installed, the new car dealership's parts department charges a mark-up of as much as 50 percent on the parts installed by the subcontractor. So there you find yet another greedy hand reaching into the pocket of the poor "grape" who has trouble with his car.

Much of the responsibility for the unfortunate situation at new car dealerships lies with the manufacturers, as mentioned earlier.

4

THOSE FRANCHISED MUFFLER, BRAKE, AND TRANSMISSION SHOPS

Turn on your television set at any time, day or night. Within a few minutes, you're sure to be watching a commercial for one of the comparatively new types of automotive supply companies which specialize in just one or two services to the motorist. It might be a household name in mufflers, brakes, or transmissions, and their familiar signs and trademarks can be found over repair shops from coast to coast. To the uninformed, it would seem that these are old established companies whose years of dedication to the public's satisfaction have resulted in deserved growth and expansion, and in one or two instances this may be so. By and large, however, one should not automatically draw this conclusion. Many of these operations are directed from just one manufacturing plant and are governed by a group of shrewd businessmen who have discovered that a million dollars worth of Madison Avenue longiloquence can familiarize the motoring public with a name and trademark more effectively today than 20 or 30 years of hard and honest dealings could before the days of the television commercial.

Those now-familiar signs and trademarks displayed over thousands of automobile repair shops have convinced the vast majority of motorists that each is part and parcel of one vast company which has grown and spread its branches after 40 or 50 years of hard-earned company growth. Nothing could be further from the truth, as a rule. The most mechanically ignorant of my readers could take over one of these establishments, no matter what his or her professional background might have been, provided he came up with the required franchise fee and agreed to the conditions laid down by the parent company. Aside from the fee, the only other stipulation in most cases would be that he buy all of his equipment, stock, and supplies from the company issuing the franchise. Thus we have an extremely misleading situation, with the gullible motorists believing that the parent company's trademark over the door means that they will be given the same high standards of quality, workmanship, and service. In reality, the million-dollar advertising budget created this mental conditioning and was carefully and skillfully designed to further some outrageous pettifoggery. As a general rule, the only similarity a motorist can expect to find between these operations is the sign over the door. The courtesies, workmanship, and values to be found inside such look-alike establishments are as different as chalk is from cheese, since they are owned and operated separately by men whose moral principles and business integrity ranges from the saintly to the downright villainous.

I must therefore warn my readers not to be overcome by the sheer amplitude of the advertising campaign; and I certainly would not recommend that you patronize any of these group advertisers as a whole. On the contrary, I must warn you that it is possible for the worst kind of crook to hide himself very nicely behind the highly respected facade provided by the company that sold him the franchise. Is it not possible that a garage proprietor who had earned a bad reputation over the years might find this kind of personal anonymity an extremely attractive business investment?

So when you need a muffler, don't start humming the strains

of the well-known jingle and drive to your nearest ———
Muffler Shop. Find out first if this particular place does a
good job. Surely someone you know will recommend it if it
does.

Please don't misunderstand me. I have nothing against the
idea of franchising, at least not when it comes to southern
fried chicken or Mother's meat pies. After all, even an untrained girl is capable of warming things like this up for us,
and we would presume that she would wash her hands with
reasonable regularity. But when it comes to installing my new
brakes or having an item fitted to my car that would prevent
poisonous gases from seeping in which might suffocate my
family or myself, then I want to know why the guy who runs
the place cannot put his own name up over the door.

The fact that this gimmick works with most people is
evidenced by the enormous prosperity these operations usually enjoy. I personally would prefer to discover a few benefits for the customer as well. Why should anyone obtain a
large amount of unearned good will on the very first day he
opens his business? I'm not sure that I want to deal with a
businessman who is either unable or unwilling to build his
own good name. How do you feel about the guy who says
that he is ——— Mufflers or ——— Transmissions, when in
fact he is really Bill Jones, who owned and operated a
hot dog stand until he recently decided that there was
more money to be made by throwing a set of brakes on
your car?

So you see, things are not always as they appear to be. No
matter what the television commercial implies, the franchised
garage does not always provide every customer with the high
standards he might expect from a company with a nationally
known name and reputation. It just means that another for-
mula for riches has been discovered by a group of very astute
businessmen, who have proved that a name and reputation
can be established after short but extremely intense advertis-

ing, and then the good will can be packaged and sold to almost anyone who can produce the franchise fee.

The franchise idea has really caught on during the past few years, and from the point of view of the investor it would seem to be the only way to fly. However, this book is aimed at the consumer and his benefit, and while the franchising idea obviously reduces the risks for a not-too-talented small business investor, I am forced to conclude that it does nothing to reduce the risk of poor quality and service to my readers, the motorists of this country. Let's face it, the whole purpose of a franchise is: first, to buy a reputation that you have not earned; secondly, to be handed a constant stream of customers by the overwhelming stream of co-op advertising put out by the parent company; and thirdly, to have an ideal solution provided for you if you are someone with the franchise fee but not too much business acumen, allowing you to follow the business stylings of a large, successful company and enjoy having just one source for everything your business needs in the way of stock, supplies, and advice.

From the customer's point of view, there is no assurance that you will be well treated at all of these establishments, or that the standards of workmanship will be similar. Whenever you drive your car in for repairs, you must hope that you are patronizing a place whose proprietor has nothing to hide behind the respected franchise facade.

I would like to make it quite clear at this point that I am not attacking the franchised garage business as a whole. There are some very fine gentlemen who choose to work under the guidance of a successful organization for many good reasons. However, my task is to protect my readers from poor quality and workmanship, and for this reason only, I must recommend that you only patronize a franchised garage for the same good reasons that you would patronize any other repair shop; because you have heard good reports from friends and associates who have been pleased with the treatment and value they have recently enjoyed at one particular establishment. And even this kind of recommendation is questionable, because these franchises often change hands overnight without any outward change of name or even staff.

Don't be too impressed, either, by the advertising pressure that insists you will save money by taking your car to the franchised garage. That television time costs an awful lot of money, and you, the customer, pay for it in the long run. Just because the man on TV says it, "it ain't necessarily so." If you really want to check out prices, first call the service department of the nearest new car dealership which sells your particular make of car and ask them how much a specific job would cost, including parts and labor. For instance, if brakes are your problem, ask what the bill would be for relining all four brakes and turning all four drums. You want the price of that and nothing else, and you don't want a reply like, "Well sir, it's going to cost you somewhere in the neighborhood of . . ." If they're honest, they can give you an exact quote simply by giving you the price of the linings and by looking up the labor time in the *Flat Rate Book*. If they refuse to give you one, then hang up and keep calling dealerships until you find one that will. Then phone the franchised garage whose advertising suggests that they will do the work for less money and ask them the same thing. Then, should less or more work be required on your brakes, at least you will know which place has the lowest rates. These phone calls will also allow you to judge for yourself which place will probably treat you best. Once you are inside one of these places, it's not the easiest thing in the world to get back in your car and leave, even if you feel that you are being pressured. There is usually a line of cars parked behind you whose owners have not read this book, and you will probably find your escape route cut off.

5

THE LARGE INDEPENDENT GARAGE

Large independents are nearly always inviting-looking places, situated on or near a main thoroughfare. Closer inspection will reveal that they have the very best and latest equipment and are generally patterned on the large new car dealership's service department. You will be met just inside the entrance by that familiar white-coated figure, the service advisor, or, as we now know him to be, the service salesman. He will listen to your troubles and then proceed to write up the repair order before asking for your signature authorizing work to commence and acknowledging your liability to pay for it in full before having your car returned to you.

Just as at the new car dealerships, a flat rate book is used to determine the amount you are going to be charged for labor. Some places may use the manufacturers' editions, while others will use the general type put out by one or two independent publishers which specialize in automotive repair manuals. Either way, you're usually going to be charged for more labor than it will take to do the job. Here, however, there are one or two rather important differences. First of all, the manager at this kind of place is usually the owner, and he is there keeping tabs on his mechanics and on the quality of the repairs he is building his reputation on. He

knows that he must compete with the local new car dealerships for your business, and he is aware that his clientele will
grow only if he can deliver something better than the competition. Therefore, he tries to build a reputation for very
high quality work at prices just a shade under those charged
at the new car dealerships. Whereas at the new car dealerships the customary pay plan for mechanics is about half of
the labor charges, the large independent will sometimes score
a lot of points over his competitors by paying his men 60
percent of the labor charges, thus attracting the very best of
the local mechanical talent and often recruiting his staff from
among the best mechanics at the local new car dealerships.

If his business premises are large enough, he will usually
have his own parts department and retail store. Most of his
parts will come from the large independent parts manufacturers, but he will always maintain an account at all of
the local new car dealerships in order to pick up in a hurry
what he needs for any particular make of car. His discount
from the new car dealership's parts department is usually
around 30 percent, while his discount from the independent
parts manufacturers will often be as much as 80 or 100 percent
of cost.

Let us now take a closer look at the kind of man who has
the temerity to challenge the franchised service departments
of the new car industry. He has to have a great deal of confidence in his ability to succeed before making the kind of
investment necessary to lease a high-priced main street location or to build his own premises. The cost of installing the
hydraulic hoists, the scopes, the compressors, and the special
lighting is just enormous.

What kind of man is this? Usually he has been a service
manager at a new car dealership and has had many years of
experience in running a large operation. He knows from this
background just what he must do to stay ahead of the competition, and he usually sets about doing it. If he is typical,

he will take a far more personal interest in you and your problem than the run of the mill service manager. He is not in the business of selling parts, nor is he forced to go along with the kind of merchandising methods set up at most new car dealership service departments by the factory representatives. This man signs the paychecks, and his presence curtails the buck-passing and time wasting that I have seen all too often at establishments whose owner or general manager rarely, if ever, risks soiling his immaculate shirt cuffs by spending much of his time in the service department.

Yes, I am recommending this type of service garage to those car owners whose vehicles are less than five years old, but I qualify this recommendation by insisting that the operation not be tied by any kind of franchise to a larger company, and that this be the only garage owned by the proprietor. My advocacy would also be contingent upon the owner sitting at the manager's desk every day and working full-time at the business. These are ideal circumstances which favor the customer, for unless the owner is a complete fool, each new client will be cherished in this competitive market, and with the owner always on the premises no effort will be spared to keep the client satisfied.

When you take your car to this type of garage, you will talk to the man whose business future depends mainly on your satisfaction. In other words, "the buck ends there." If the work that his mechanics perform and the prices he charges are only on a par with the new car dealership's standards, he will make little or no headway, because people are understandably attracted to the garage which displays their car's name above the door. Motorists usually carry all of the mental ridges carved by years and years of the automobile manufacturers' advertising, and they react subconsciously but favorably to such time-worn and fallacious phrases as "factory tools" and "factory trained mechanics." Many of us are even inclined to the belief that only the mechanics at the new car dealership will really understand our car, and that other garages will be forced to improvise with tools that will not properly fit the part and with mechanics who, because they choose not to describe themselves as factory trained, will take longer to find and correct the problem.

In the past, I have been associated with new car dealerships whose service departments were, in my opinion, a disgrace to the automobile trade. In spite of daily complaints and even court actions taken against them by irate customers, they continued to prosper, because they were able to hide their true image behind the respected trademark of the manufacturer. The large independent garage owner does not have this mask of respectability to hide any of his employees' inefficiencies. In today's repair business, he would not survive for six months if he were unable to combat with sheer quality and honest value the millions of advertising dollars spent every year by the manufacturers and the franchised muffler and transmission outlets.

To further refine my recommendation of the large independent repair garage, there is one easily detectable giveaway I would warn you to watch out for and try to avoid: *the white-coated service salesman.* At the large independent garage, he might have a different purpose, but then again he might not. In any event, I never have and never will like the idea of a commissioned salesman approaching me when I'm having trouble with my car, a man whose only aim is to earn as high a commission as he can from my predicament. At such a time, I want a skilled mechanic to listen to my troubles and then to examine my car. When he satisfies himself that he has found the cause of my problem, I want him to tell me first what it is, secondly, how long it will take him to fix it, and thirdly, how much it's going to cost me.

If any garage owner would care to try and tell me why a service customer should not be given this kind of straightforward treatment, I would be a most interested listener. Let him beware however, if he attempts to dish out any of the nonsense that I have heard customers given during the past 20 years or so. It would seem to me that the only way to conduct a good customer-oriented garage would be for each customer to be encouraged to establish a good first-name relationship with a mechanic whose work and skills he had tested over a long period and on whom he knew he could depend for an honest appraisal of his needs. Once this relationship had been attained, surely the mechanic and his employer would have a customer for life; certainly they would as far as this writer is concerned. I do not enjoy being greeted by a service salesman who does not get in the car with me and show his skill and qualifications as an *advisor* by diagnosing my car's troubles then and there and advising me on the best and most economical solution to them. I just don't like the service salesman system. I never have and I never will . . .

At the kind of large independent garage that I would recommend, the service salesman would not be endured. The man who greets the customer would be either the garage owner himself or his chief service manager, working directly under the supervision of the proprietor. Either of these gentlemen would surely be a skilled automobile mechanic with a comprehensive knowledge of automobile problems and both the motive and the ability to tell me honestly what it's going to take to put my car back in good shape once again. I want him to be the boss, who will profit from my continued patronage, not just a personable young man whose commission vouchers for that week depend upon his skill at conning unfortunate motorists into agreeing to pay for unnecessary repairs and replacements.

Remember, then, at the best places you will not be forced to deal with a service salesman, service writer, service advisor, or whatever else he may call himself in order to cover up his real purpose. Take your car to the large independent which complies with the few qualifications I have specified in this chapter. If you can find such a place in your area, then count yourself as one of the more fortunate motorists, and look no further for your car's service requirements.

6

THE SMALL ONE- OR
TWO-MAN GARAGE

The automobile mechanic who has the temerity to open a one-man repair shop today and compete with the new car dealerships and those multi-limbed franchised garages with their vast advertising budgets must be blessed with both a great deal of moxey and the self-confidence that only goes with the knowledge that he has something to offer the motoring public.

Have you noticed that the giants are not having much success in putting the small one-man auto repair shop out of business? Despite the millions spent on advertising their services and the prime locations they occupy in every city and town, they have hardly made a dent in the number of small repair shops across the country—and it is my opinion that they never will.

You will recall my criticism of today's mechanics at the larger operations: they are usually men who have undergone a short training period in which they have learned just one or two tasks which require little knowledge other than how to remove an old part and replace it with a new one. I'm afraid that this type of training would not hold up in the one-man repair shop. Here, the term "R & R" does not mean remove and replace, it usually means remove and repair. Whereas in the multi-stalled garage if your car was in for a brake reline and a tune-up it would be worked on by two different mechanics in two different stalls, here at the small garage there is only one stall as a rule, and certainly the man who gives your car a tune-up is more than capable of installing the new brake linings.

If your car is at least five years old, it's probably pretty well worn out by today's standards. You've heard of planned obsolescence, surely? Therefore, if you dared to take it to a service department which employed the service salesman, your ultimate bill would probably come to more than the old car was worth. Besides this, the fact that you are driving a car that is more than five years old suggests that you probably could not afford to pay for any costly major overhauls. There are many millions of people in this country in this situation, and as a general rule, it is these individuals who make up the clientele of the many one-man repair shops that still flourish.

Here, then, is the difference between the modern, well-equipped, multi-stalled garage and the somewhat shabby workshop where a highly skilled, all-around automobile mechanic offers his experience and know-how for sale. His overhead is practically nothing when compared to his more ostentatious competitors. He has no advertising budget to take care of, no office staff to pay, and the rent is always very low. Thus, he is able to charge $3 or $4 an hour less for his labor than the garage with all of the expensive fol-de-rols. He also knows that his customers cannot afford to patronize the larger places and that he will only retain their custom by charging a lot less for his services than his more "mouthy" competitors. Probably more than half of the parts he uses will come from the local car wrecking yards, and don't disparage him for this. Cars that have been involved in accidents are towed into the wrecker's yard with plenty of mechanical parts that were in no way affected by the collision, and these are sold to individuals with enough know-how to tell the good ones from the no-good ones. The wrecking yard's best customers are without a doubt the local used car dealers and the one-man repair shops. When you drive your car into a large repair shop with a worn-out wheel bearing or differential, you are going to be sold a new unit from their parts department. Our friend the all-around mechanic with his own little garage caters to the people who have to watch each dollar, and by getting most of the parts he needs from the wreckers, he can cut your parts bill by more than half without in any way giving you an inferior value.

You must have noticed that I mentioned the used car dealers as being good customers of the wrecking yards. I should add here that those dealers that specialize in buying and selling cars that are four years old or older are usually very good customers at the one-man repair shops, too. So don't knock the local one-man repair shop. You'll have to admit that your local used car dealer knows a little more about cars than you, and every one of them that I have known uses the local one-man garage for low-cost, reliable car repairs.

I suppose the main difference between this type of small operation and the large multi-stalled garage can be found in the motives behind each procedure. Whereas at most of the new car dealerships and the independents they are kept busy replacing everything with new parts and going all out to beat the *Flat Rate Book* time allowances, at the one-man shop the owner knows that he must save his customers money on their repair bills in order to retain their patronage. Can you imagine how many million spark plugs are thrown in the trash can every day at new car dealerships? Plugs that only need sanding and resetting to be perfectly good spark plugs again. At most of the places that I have been connected with, when a mechanic is handed a repair order which includes a tune-up, he will go to the parts counter and draw a set of spark plugs, a set of points, and a condenser before he has even taken the old ones out and checked them. Thousands upon thousands of condensers are thrown away every day and new ones are charged to the customer, even though one condenser will usually last the entire life of any automobile. You've all had starter trouble at one time or another and been relieved when informed that you just needed a new solenoid switch. Here again, thousands of perfectly good solenoid starter switches are thrown away each day after only half of their usefulness is gone.

It is here that our friend the all-around automobile mechanic who has been taught his trade well can and will save you lots of money. He secretly despises the "R & R" men with their skimpy few weeks of training. He knows that most of them have probably never even opened up a solenoid switch to find out how it works, and it is here that he is rightfully proud of his own skills and experience. No part of any car is a mystery to him, and he wouldn't even consider buying and installing a new part before he was satisfied that the old one was worn out completely. His equipment includes items that many of today's so-called mechanics would find completely mystifying. Items like turning lathes and micrometers are not to be found in the abbreviated cirriculum at the capsulized mechanic's training centers which seem to be springing up all over the place today. Please understand that it would be impossible to generalize with certainty about whether a part could be repaired more economically than it could be replaced. This would naturally depend on the amount of wear and tear and the cost of the replacement part. What I am saying is that this kind of good judgment is never used except at the small one-man garage, where the artisan only survives by performing his daily work with standards of skill and contrived economy that are unheard of at the large, volume-minded establishments.

Let us take that one example of the starter solenoid switch. For those among you that do not even know what function it performs, let me describe it very briefly for you. Simply stated, a solenoid switch is a small wired coil that creates a strong magnetic field whenever you turn your key in the starter switch. Acting just like a toy magnet, it simply pulls the two starter contacts together and connects the battery to your starter motor. The contact itself is simply a small round washer made of brass or copper. When you think of how many times you start your car in a couple of years, you will realize that this little washer takes quite a beating in time. The side of it which actually makes the contact gradually becomes more and more pitted, until one morning when you turn your key in the starter all you hear is a faint "click, click." This means that there just isn't enough smooth surface left on the side of the washer to make a satisfactory connection. Go to any new car dealership, gas station, or large independent with this problem, and without hesitation they will simply remove the entire solenoid unit and install a new one. Your bill will amount to between $10 and $25, depending on where you take your car. If you are lucky enough to have found yourself a good all-around mechanic, he will simply take out that little pitted washer and replace it with a new one, or better still, he might just turn the old one around so that the unused side of it faces the contact, thus doubling the life of your solenoid switch. For this little piece of know-how and old-fashioned experience, your bill might be all of $2, maybe even $3 if he's greedy.

How many new solenoid switches do you suppose are sold every year? Many hundreds of thousands, I'm sure. Don't you think the new car manufacturers would set up a loud howl if their dealers' mechanics started doing things like this? If you don't, then you certainly don't know them very well. Imagine having their new solenoid sales cut by 50 percent! Then again, there's the new car dealer's parts department to consider. It would seem that having a few good old-fashioned automobile mechanics around would certainly cut their volume of business. Just imagine having guys down in the shop who repaired and adjusted parts of cars. What would happen if the mechanics started rewiring generators, repairing solenoid switches, and sanding and adjusting those millions of spark plugs which they throw away every day? Just imagine giving a car a tune-up without replacing the perfectly good condenser with a new one from the parts department. If this state of affairs were brought about by our insistence on better-trained mechanics, we'd have all of the parts department managers in the nation climbing the walls of their comfortable offices. They'd have to change their style and get back to the real free enterprise system, just like the guy in the small, one-man shop who sweats every day in order to compete with their voracious merchandising methods.

These examples of unnecessary expense charged to the motoring public are just a few taken at random. There are thousands of parts that go to make up an automobile, many of which are discarded by service departments long before their usefulness is exhausted. The solenoid switches, the spark plugs and condensers are just a few of the many parts that could be repaired instead of being replaced, if they were serviced by a properly trained and skilled artisan whose motive was to build a regular clientele in his immediate zone of influence. This man's local reputation is hard-earned and well deserved. Not for him a down payment to a franchise house for a ready-made reputation. He just sticks up his sign over the door and waits for someone with something more than mechanical problems to stop by. His drop-in customers are usually the owners of older cars trying to find repairs for less money than they would be charged at the larger and fancier places: in other words, people with two problems, one mechanical and one financial.

While I have a great admiration for the one-man repair shop and all that it represents, I am certainly not suggesting that from now on you take your car there for all of its needed repairs. There are some limitations to what a small shop can do, especially when it comes to the use of very expensive equipment that is usually only available at the more prosperous establishments. All the same, if you feel that you are being "R & R'ed" out of existence by your present service garage, you might give him a try the next time your car starts to act up, especially if it's an older car no longer covered by the manufacturer's warranty. You might just be lucky and discover that you have met a mechanical genius, and he'll certainly do his darnedest to please you and keep you as a customer.

I recall an incident which took place many years ago, long before I was able to afford a late model car. I forget the make and even the year of the car I was driving, but I do remember that it was pretty old. There I was on my way home one afternoon, when without warning the old car began to splutter and miss badly. I think I had about $6 in my jeans, and I was planning to spend two of those precious dollars at the next available gas station. Quite by chance the engine finally expired right outside a small one-man auto repair shop. Not too hopefully, I entered the rather dingy and very greasy little hole in the wall and explained my predicament to the old guy who crawled out from under the old pickup truck which almost filled the workshop. I also told him that I didn't have more than $4 or $5 at the most that I could give him right then, but I'd be glad to give him the rest of what I would owe him out of my next paycheck. He agreed to take a look, and after a minute or two with his head under the hood of my car he emerged triumphantly with my distributor cap in his hand.

"Here's your trouble." He pointed to a small crack in the bakelite, and I breathed a sigh of relief, as I knew that even my limited funds would buy a new cap. He asked me again how much money I had, and when I told him that I was limited to no more than $5, he gave me a kindly grin and told me to follow him back into his shop. He wrapped part of the distributor cap in a dirty old rag before gently gripping it in the metal vise on his workbench. Then, using an old hand drill, he drilled a tiny hole right through the center of the crack. As he worked he explained to me that what was causing my engine to misfire was that a crack in a distributor cap gradually collects dust and carbons. These then collect dampness from the atmosphere and eventually act just like a wire running from one distributor point to another, causing a direct short. By drilling a small hole right through the crack, he was in fact cutting this wire just as though he had used a pair of wire cutters. Sure enough, when he clipped the cap back on my car and told me to start the engine it fired up right away and ran smoother than I had ever known it to before. I never did have to replace that distributor cap, and I owned that car for more than a year with that little hole drilled by an old guy with mechanical know-how who was not out to take advantage of a young guy with car troubles. Oh, by the way, he charged me one whole dollar for one of the most valuable lessons I have ever been given on the art of repair and replacement. For my dollar, I had purchased about five minutes of his labor—and a whole lifetime of his experience and pride in his skill.

So, the next time you drive past a small repair garage, don't sneer at its run-down appearance and its lop-sided sign. That old saying that you can't tell a book by its cover certainly applies to the automobile repair business. Certainly some of the most infamous rascals in our business hide themselves and their true purposes behind a nice gilded facade of respectability. Of course, you must appreciate that all one-man repair shops do not house the kind of mechanical skill I have been telling you about, but many of them do; and if your car is getting along in years and you have to watch your budget carefully, then it might be well worth your while to try and find this kind of inexpensive service in your locality. Perhaps the best method of finding a good one would be to enquire at one or two of your local used car dealers, especially those that sell the older type of clean-looking automobiles. These establishments usually send their work out to the best and most inexpensive small repair shop in the area, and if there is a mechanical genius in their neighborhood you can bet that they will find him sooner or later.

If you are not getting good, reasonably priced car repairs where you now take your car, it might be worth your while to give your local one-man operation a try. On the other hand, if your present service department is doing a good and satisfactory job for you, then stay with them and count yourself among the lucky ones. There is nothing better than a large, well-equipped, well-staffed service department, provided it does not become an avaricious monster that is more interested in bleeding the customer than in bleeding the customer's brakes.

One last word about the small one-man garage. If you enjoy being buttered up by the suave, white-coated "service advisor" and you prefer to sit in a comfortable waiting room watching color television while your car is being serviced, then you should stay away from the kind of disreputable-looking operation I have been describing. His hands will most certainly be dirty, and his waiting room will probably be the coffee shop across the street; but you'll be greeted by the owner of the business, a man who is genuinely grateful to you for stopping by and giving him an opportunity to demonstrate his skills. He'll do all he can to impress you, not only with his good work, but also by showing you how you can save money by becoming one of his regular customers.

7

CAR REPAIRS AT GAS STATIONS

Every time I look the other way for a moment, it seems that one of the major oil companies has purchased another corner at an intersection and is installing a new gas station, much to the chagrin of the unfortunate guy who has sunk his hard-earned savings into one of the other gas stations across the street. How on earth do they all make a living? That's easy. They sell gas, tires, batteries, wiper blades, and . . . they repair cars.

Let us take the closest look you have ever taken at the gas station business as it now is in this country. Even the oil companies themselves would be forced to admit that there is no longer any real money to be earned by the guy who invests a few grand of his own in a gas station and just pumps gasoline for a living. Part and parcel of today's gas station business is servicing automobiles and doing some repairs. Today's gas station is built with at least two repair stalls and one hoist, to say nothing of special display racks for tire sales and other accessories. Few of them do not have a prominent sign which indicates that there is a mechanic on duty; and how many of us, at one time or another, have not been glad to patronize this gentleman, especially when every other garage in the area was closed up for the day?

Like so many things about the automobile business, the word "service" is overused and no longer bears any relationship to the truth. Most of us are busy at our jobs between the hours of eight in the morning and five in the evening, right? And where are our cars during these hours? Parked outside our places of employment, right? When do most of us use our automobiles? Getting to and from work, during the evenings, and on weekends if we're typical. Now, when do the new car dealerships make their so-called service available to us? With the exception of one evening (almost always Monday), their repair garages are open from eight in the morning until five in the evening. Cars usually give us very little trouble while they are parked outside our places of business, but oh boy, can they be a headache after five o'clock and on weekends. Understandably, therefore, it's a proven fact that when we need a mechanic, the only place we can find one as a rule is by pulling in at a gas station. You can buy a new car at almost any dealership until late at night and all through the weekend, but if you are in need of some service for that same car, you must take time off from work and bring it in to the dealership during office hours.

It would seem that millions of dollars worth of car repair and service business is being passed up by the new car dealerships and allowed to be gratefully swallowed up by the many thousands of gas stations whose services are made available to the motoring public seven days a week and usually around the clock. It just doesn't make sense that about two-thirds of all of the service and repair business in the United States is shrugged off in this manner. Can you see the relationship between this and my earlier contention that the manufacturers have the new car dealers by the throat so tightly that he is compelled to obey their slightest whim? Picture with me, if you can, a new car dealer with integrity, who suggests to the manufacturer that he attempt to give good service to the motoring public by keeping his service department open late every night and on weekends. I can see the hands around the dealer's throat tighten as the manufacturer reminds him what the new car business is really about.

"Sell cars! Our production lines must be kept going all out. Get those salesmen on the ball and make them sell cars. Pay them on commission only; if they don't sell cars, let them starve. Service? We don't make any money out of service. If you start giving the public good service, they might even keep their cars for another year before trading them in on new ones! Then where would we be? Why, that would cost us millions. Close that service department at five o'clock sharp and never open it on Saturdays or Sundays.

"No, no, not the sales departments; keep the car salesmen there all night if you can. It doesn't cost you or us anything to keep them on duty every evening and on weekends, 'cause they're on commission only, right? Your reputation? Your integrity? Hey, which would you rather have, a lot of integrity or a lot of money? Come on, buddy, climb aboard the bandwagon. After all, if the poor schnook can't get his car fixed, he's more likely to trade it in on a new one, isn't he? Get smart, or you'll never make it in this business."

That's the picture I get after almost a quarter of a century of being in the profession.

Now, getting back to my ideas about gas station repairs. It has been my belief for a long time now that where big business is concerned, our free enterprise system no longer exists. The competition would appear to be there, with gas stations on almost every street corner, but there never seems to be any competition where price is concerned. You drive through one town and the price of premium gasoline at all of the major oil companies' outlets is 38.9¢ per gallon. At the next town, the price is uniformly 36.9¢ per gallon. Notice please that, to within one tenth of a penny, their prices are the same. Should one enterprising gas station operator attempt to bring a little of the good old American system back into the business by reducing his prices by one miserable cent a gallon, signs begin to appear at every gas station in town screaming "PRICE WAR!" I can imagine the poor guy being branded as some kind of a red radical for his impudence. Oh boy, what would our forefathers have said? Certainly, with this kind of price-fixing the price of tea wouldn't have caused such a commotion in Boston back in the days of those red radicals, would it?

Gas station operators do not really compete with each other where the selling of gasoline is concerned, even if some of the dumber ones still believe that they do. They are there just to provide a readily accessible outlet for the enormous gasoline production refineries that the major oil companies now own, just as the new car dealers are in existence primarily to dispose of the greatly increased production now made possible by new automated facilities. The new car dealers now make their real profits through their parts and service departments, and the gasoline station operators make their real profits by selling tires, batteries, oil additives, and . . . automobile repairs.

Besides the gas stations that are leased on a franchise arrangement from the major oil companies, there are others which are called the independents. Just as you might expect in a society where all men are born equal, but some are more equal than others, where the independent gas stations are concerned things are not always what they seem to be. In other words, many "independents" are not independent at all, but are in fact owned by a major oil company or one of its subsidiaries in order that its stale gasoline can be disposed of without bespoiling the good reputation of its trade brand name. Unlike wine and whisky, gasoline does not improve with aging. It is produced in enormous quantities every day and stored in those arena-like tanks you have all seen surrounding the oil refineries. The multitude of tanker trucks that keep the gas stations supplied fill up at these storage tanks daily, where a careful check is kept to see that the octane value of the stored gasoline is no lower than that claimed for it. Because of this prodigious system of gasoline storage, there is always a tank that gets down to one-quarter full or less. At this stage, the tanker trucks usually take no more from this tank, but move on to the next full tank. Although many thousands of gallons still remain in the quarter-full storage tank, because of its age and the possibility of sucking up some of the sediment which will always sink to the bottom of a storage tank, the name brand gasoline manufacturers can no longer guarantee either its purity or its octane value. Rather than let it be wasted, they distribute it through the so-called independents at a reduced price. Certainly if you have ever pulled into a gasoline station that sells an unfamiliar brand of gasoline at a "bargain" price, the chances are that soon after leaving there your engine lost some of its efficiency and began to "ping" as you pressed on the accelerator pedal. You may also have experienced some carburetor troubles during the weeks following the good deal you made on a tankful of gasoline at an independent gas station. This kind of trouble may well have been caused by the small amount of sediment that you may have received as a bonus for patronizing the lower-priced independent.

I have found that there *is* a way to get a good buy on good gasoline. It is becoming quite common now for the nationally known multi-branch department stores to have their own gas stations built on to their customer parking facilities. Now, companies like Sears-Roebuck, White Front Stores, and Zody's are not about to be sold stale gasoline by anyone. Their many outlets can distribute such an enormous amount of gasoline every day that they have become among the most important customers the major oil companies have. Even though they display their own signs at their gas stations and indicate that the brand of gasoline they sell is their own, the truth is that they obtain their supplies from one or another of the major brand refineries, and they certainly would only accept the genuine article: gasoline from the full storage tanks, which is exactly the same as that supplied to the name brand gas stations. At my local branch of Sears-Roebuck, the cars are usually lined up for half a block waiting to get to the gas pumps, where perfectly good gasoline is usually on sale for anywhere from 6¢ to 10¢ a gallon less than at the name brand stations across the street. I always buy my gasoline there and recommend it to all of my readers.

There are, of course, still some independent gas stations that really are independent, stations owned outright by the operator, who buys his gasoline from whomever he wishes. The chances are that the gasoline on sale here will be perfectly good and competitively priced. My apologies to these fine gentlemen if my last remarks seem to be unfair to them. Unfortunately, this type of gasoline station is rapidly joining the buffalo and the old-fashioned type of new car dealership as nothing more than a nostalgic memory.

Gasoline company credit cards are also worthy of mention here. These are probably the main reason the major oil companies don't have to compete price-wise where their gasoline outlets are concerned. I have never used one, and those that have been sent to me have always been promptly returned to wherever they came from. A $10 bill takes up no more room in my billfold than a gas credit card. So, where most people now keep their card, I keep my $10 bill, and do you know what?—the service station attendants accept my $10 bill just as readily as they do a gasoline credit card. They really do! Do you know something else? My $10 bill is also accepted at Sears-Roebuck gas stations, and this allows me to get a better deal on gasoline than my neighbor whose wallet is just bulging with all kinds of credit cards.

Now, what about those car repairs at gas stations? It just isn't possible for me to give you a general recommendation about them, because there are so many of them with so many standards of skill and so many motives for being there. At some stations, there might be just a couple of young guys who enjoy messing around with cars, while at others you can find a top-class mechanic who puts in a few extra hours evenings and weekends in order to supplement the income he makes as a mechanic at one of the local new car dealerships. Let me just say this in favor of all of the many thousands of gas stations that keep a mechanic on duty late at night and weekends: what on earth would we do without them? At least here there is some meaning to the word service. At least here you will get some kind of help when you need it outside of office hours. I would like the manufacturers and the dealerships to stop even using the word service in their advertisements, because very few of them even attempt to provide it to their customers. The best I can say about gas station mechanics is that, in almost every case, they are quite capable of providing valuable assistance after five in the afternoons and on weekends when nothing better is available. They can give your car an oil change and a lubrication, repair a flat tire, install a sealed beam unit in your headlamp, change your wiper blades, and perhaps fit a new set of shock absorbers. For the rest of your repairs, you should take your car to the garages that are the busiest in your neighborhood, for it will be there, where the most money can be earned, that you will surely find the best mechanics and the best equipment.

If you are fortunate enough to find a service station that sublets its hoist and repair stall to a *full-time* mechanic, though, you may have found one of those geniuses that I described in chapter 7, and you should look no further for any repairs that you need. Cases like this, however, are the exception rather than the rule, and you should check him out carefully before placing too much confidence in his abilities.

8

DIAGNOSTIC ANALYSIS CENTERS

Back in 1956, I was employed as the general sales manager of a large Chevrolet-Oldsmobile dealership in Ontario, Canada, just outside the fine city of Toronto. Canada is divided into provinces, just as this country is divided into states, and it was at about this time that the Province of Ontario opened its first automobile Diagnostic Center. This was operated by the provincial government and directed by the department of motor vehicles, using funds appropriated from the road fund taxes and the gasoline taxes.

There were no profit motives involved, and certainly no repairs of any kind were available at the center. It was just a wonderful idea that was voted into law by a group of fine legislators whose only motive was to make the streets and highways of Ontario much safer for both the motorists and the pedestrians. I visited the center at my first opportunity and was most impressed by what I saw. As I recall, it covered the equivalent of two city blocks, and motorists entered at a gate where, at that time, they paid $2 for the service of having their car electronically analyzed by very high-paid automotive scientists using the most fabulous and costly devices. Each motorist was given a two-page statement which gave an accurate report on the efficiency and condition of each section of his car, based on a safety and efficiency rating of 100. Any areas of the car which were found to have a rating low enough to be considered unsafe by these experts were given a rating printed in red; this automatically required the owner of the car to return with it within 21 days, at which time it either received a satisfactory rating or had its license plates removed and returned to the Department of Motor Vehicles.

Any vehicles that were stopped by a police officer and found to be suspect insofar as their safety was concerned were automatically cited, and a notice was handed to the operator requiring him to produce the diagnostic center's report on the vehicle within ten days at the local police station. This whole idea worked out so well that I have often wondered why, with our enormous number of traffic accidents, we could not find the funds to set up similar centers throughout this country.

Understandably, therefore, when I first read that automobile diagnostic centers were beginning to spring up in the United States, I was delighted and anxious to find one and see how it compared with the old Canadian idea. I expected to find quite a display of sophisticated equipment, and possibly some of the latest devices that have been developed during this new age of space technology. After all, it had been some 13 years since I had seen what Canada had to offer, and I felt sure that I would find evidence of the enormous strides that have been made in this field since 1956.

I obtained the address of the center in my area and took an afternoon off from work in order to have sufficient time to have a good look around the place. When I got to the address I had been given, I just couldn't locate the center. Remembering how large and imposing-looking the Canadian place was, I naturally was on the lookout for at least a block-long building. All I found at the address I had been given was a small service repair garage. Then I saw the newly painted sign that had been put up outside the entrance to this garage.

I had found the American version of an automobile diagnostic center. I only stepped inside long enough to see the
three service stalls and the three mechanics working on cars,
just like the employees of any other garage. There was a
waiting room, and I stepped in there long enough to pick up
a couple of brochures about the analysis and diagnostic service, which was available there for a fee of $18 for eight-
cylinder cars and $14.95 for cars with six-cylinder engines.

Somehow I could smell "come-on" the whole time I was in
there, and later, as I sat outside in my car reading the brochures, I felt myself getting angrier by the minute. The car
I was driving that day was almost new, and I certainly didn't
want anyone in that place messing it up, so I decided to
check the place out later by bringing back an older car after
I had had it checked out by one of the best automobile engineers I know. Only by comparing his report with the $18 re-
port I would get at this place would I be in a position to report fairly on the new diagnostic centers that were being
promoted to the long-suffering motorists as some kind of gift
from heaven.

As I write this, I have in front of me the brochures I was
given. Leaving out only the name and address of this particular establishment, here is the complete wording on each brochure:

An Auto Analysts Electronic-Dyno Tune-Up
Is So Much More Complete

18 separate steps instead of the conventional 7 are included.

It starts with the technician removing the entire distributor from
the engine, not just the cap.

Then, in addition to removing the spark plugs, we:

Test centrifugal and vacuum advance mechanisms, replacing
defective parts.

Check and adjust the alignment of the points and the tension of the spring.

Install a new condenser. [Oh, boy . . . and that's my only comment.]

Place the entire distributor in a special strobograph machine, set the points, and run in for approximately 30 minutes.

Check the distributor advance curve so that it matches the specifications for your make and model of car.

Lubricate cam lobe, make final adjustment on dwell setting.

Reinstall the entire distributor.

Clean, test, and reset gap or replace spark plugs if required.

Check battery cables and clean terminals.

Clean air filter and engine top, replace element if required.

Drive car on chassis dynamometer and connect all the instrument leads.

Run car on dyno at various speeds to balance carburetor and set idle speed.

Run car on dyno and set ignition timing under load for maximum engine performance.

Check complete ignition system operation under road load conditions.

Then, in very large bold type, the brochure states: "ONLY $15," adding (in very tiny type) "for 4 & 6 cyl. cars." In even tinier type, next comes "$18 for 8 cyl." Then, incredibly, they found some even tinier type, which, if you focus your eyesight carefully, reads: "plus parts as required."

Despite the first statement on the brochure, that 18 separate steps are taken instead of the customary seven, I can count only 16 listed in the brochure. Perhaps they forgot to include 17, the mechanic picking up his screwdriver, and

18, the mechanic putting his screwdriver down again. I wonder how they would list the seven separate steps used by other garages.

On the back page of the brochure is the following:
YOUR ENGINE WILL REALLY SING . . . with an AUTO ANALYSTS
ELECTRONIC-DYNO TUNE-UP . . . because . . .

You made AUTO ANALYSTS your diagnostician—WHY NOT THE SURGEON.

SKILLED specialists following the diagnostic report know exactly what to fix.

QUALITY CONTROL—All repairs are re-tested after completion to assure satisfaction.

WRITTEN GUARANTEE on all jobs. Only our expert workmanship, top quality parts, and quality control re-check make this possible.

FREE RE-CHECK. Bring your car back for a re-check within a 2-week period. No appointment necessary.

INSTANT CREDIT is available. No down payment and up to 24 months to pay. Or use any major credit card.

YET WITH ALL THIS, AUTO ANALYSTS REPAIRS COST NO MORE.

It's sad but true, I'm afraid, that what promised to be a gigantic step forward for the many motorists in this country turned out to be nothing more than just another example of the old shell game. I take particular objection to this idea, though, because it is obviously designed to mislead the public into believing that they will be given an unbiased and completely honest report on the condition of their cars. Not only is this a disgusting method of blackmailing the uninformed motorist into having his repairs done at the diagnostic garage, they even have the unadulterated cheek to charge $18 just to give the automobile the kind of cursory check that would gladly be given without charge at any decent repair shop.

Before I tell you what happened to me when I took a perfectly nice little used car through one of these analysis shops, let me reprint here the wording on the other brochure I was given. The only words not included are the name and address of the outfit. Perhaps one day one of these rascals will be dumb enough to challenge my conclusions during one of my radio and television tours across the country. I look forward to getting his reaction to the many scam documents I was given during several of my anonymous visits to these establishments. Here now is the second brochure:

DON'T LET THIS HAPPEN TO YOU!

REPAIR ORDER

Name _____John Doe_____

Address _____Anywhere_____

_____

Replace Automatic Transmission
_____

_____

$236.80.
_____

_____

_____

_____

That's the front page of the brochure. Then, inside, it reads:

HAVE YOUR AUTOMATIC TRANSMISSION SERVICED REGULARLY.

The automatic transmission in today's automobile is an extremely complicated piece of mechanism which requires regular servicing and oil changes just as with the engine. It consists of several hundred parts that must function as a unit for trouble-free performance. Under normal operation, temperatures as high as 350 degrees cause varnish to form and the same type of sludge which collects in your engine also develops in your transmission. This is the primary cause of the malfunction and breakdown of the unit.

Regular servicing of your transmission (which could be more costly to replace or repair than the engine) will prevent most of the problems that occur and eliminate power losses which can reach 50% at low speeds. Because of the moisture condensation which causes the fluid to foam and the contamination, the oil should be changed and the filter screen cleaned every 10,000 to 15,000 miles, dependent upon the operation of the vehicle. Careful adherence to this regular service program will add thousands of carefree miles to your car.

6-POINT TRANSMISSION SERVICE SPECIAL.

Drain oil, remove and clean pan and screen.

Carefully inspect all visible working parts.

Adjust bands according to manufacturer's specifications using special precision tools.

Replace clean screen, check pan for dents on edges between bolt holes, install new gaskets, and reinstall pan on transmission.

Fill with ———— Hydraulic Oil according to the manufacturer's instructions for the individual make and model car.

Road test to check operation and shift pattern. Make any minor adjustments necessary for smooth operation.

$14.95 Complete including labor and fluid.

Then, on the back page of this brochure, is the following:

WATCH FOR THESE DANGER SIGNS.

The early correction of any of these danger signals can save you as much as $400 in repairs.

* Any unusual noise.
* The odor of hot oil or excess heat under the floor boards.
* Slipping or jerking operation.
* Uneven shift pattern.

* Sticking in one gear.
* An unusual amount of vibration.
* Oil in the driveway or parking area.

Our service personnel have been especially trained to service your automatic transmission, and remember, an ounce of prevention is worth a pound of cure.

Then, at the very bottom of the page, is the trademark and symbol of a nationally known company which is an association of automatic transmission rebuilders.

All of this service selling comes from an organization that advertises only its diagnostic service. Simply reading the brochures convinced me that here was a new scam if ever I'd seen one. Yet, when I arrived at the first center with my perfectly good little three-year-old Chevvy, it was doing gangbusters business. Anyway, I paid my $18, and instead of sitting in the waiting room for my car to be checked, I asked if I could go into the service area and take a look around. I was grudgingly given permission to do so, probably because I looked just like any other know-nothing tire kicker.

What I found inside was a plain, ordinary, small service garage equipped with less testing gear than could be found in any decent repair shop. One stall had a hoist; another did have an oscilloscope and a dynamometer, but these are standard equipment everywhere nowadays. The third stall appeared to have no special purpose, and as I approached it its occupant emerged screaming expletives which certainly could not be printed here. He had apparently just removed a small portion of his thumb and was beseeching someone to find a Band-aid for him in, to use his own words, "this God-forsaken hole."

After I had been in the shop for about half an hour, my car was driven into the stall with the hoist. After it had been raised high enough for the attendant to walk under it, he walked around underneath it with a trouble lamp in his hand, tugging on the drive shaft and sounding out a few places with his hammer. Every now and then he walked over to his work bench and wrote something down on what appeared to be a repair order. When he was through, the hoist was lowered and my car was moved into the next stall, and I watched while an ordinary everyday tune-up diagnosis was performed. Nothing special was done, and no special equipment was used. Every modern repair shop uses the same method of checking out a car's ignition system when it is in for a tune-up.

Fifteen minutes later, I was summoned into what I immediately recognized as the closing room, and there, sitting at his desk, was my old friend the T. O. man. For those of you who haven't read my book, *What You Should Know Before You Buy a Car*, I'd better explain that the T. O. man is the supersalesman who Takes Over the deal from the inept and fumbling greeter salesman and really puts it to you. He is always introduced to the customer as the manager and usually has the word "manager" painted on his office door.

Having spent several of my 25 years in the car business as a T. O. man, I always enjoy watching and listening to a good one working at his trade, and in this instance I was not disappointed.

After motioning me into the seat facing the window, so that the sunlight would place me at some disadvantage, he sat for one whole minute staring morosely at the report on my car's condition. Then, with the kind of sigh that a doctor must give just before telling a patient with a terminal illness that it would be best if he didn't renew any of his magazine subscriptions, he leaned over and handed me the report.

Let me point out at this stage that the car I had brought with me had been carefully prepared for this test by an automotive consultant engineer with the highest credentials. His background included 12 years as service manager with a well-respected new car dealership in Southern California, and for the past four years, up to and including the time this book is being written, he has been a teacher of automotive engineering at one of the better known institutes of technology. The car we had chosen was a three-year-old Chevrolet in exceptionally nice condition mechanically. My engineer friend had spent the previous afternoon going over the car himself and bringing it up to its peak condition. When I had called to collect the car from his workshop that morning, he had told me that it was in pretty good condition considering that it was three years old, and that the only item of any importance which he would attend to if it were his car would be two brake linings and a small leak welded at the top of the radiator.

Here now is the report that was handed to me by the man in the white coat sitting across from me at his desk. It is an exact copy and everything on it should be self-explanatory with the exception of the notations I've marked with an asterisk. I have no idea what these symbols mean, but it is my theory that they represent coded information that is of some value to the T. O. Man.

UNDER HOOD INSPECTION   STATION I

Condition Code: S = Satisfactory   R = Repair   AJ = Adjust
SE = Service   RE = Replace   !! = Severe   * = Critical.

	Comments	Cond.	Parts	Labor
1. Engine Oil.		S		
2. Trans. Oil.		RE	11.00	12.50
3. Radiator Cap.		RE	1.95	NC
4. Coolant Level.	I 32*	SE	6.80	NC
5. Cool Syst. Test.	Flush.	SE		
6. Radiator Cond.	Upper Seam.	R		27.00
7. U. L. Rad. & He. Hoses.		S		
8. Belts		S		
9. Thermo. Fan.		—		
10. Air Filter.		RE	4.50	NC
11. Fuel Filter.		S		

	Comments	Cond.	Parts	Labor
12. Choke Valve Oper.		S		
13. Fuel System Ck.		S		
14. Eng. Steam Clean.		SE		6.00
15. Head Gask. Test.		S		
16. Smog Valve (PCV)	Pressure.	SE		3.50
17. Air Cond.		—		
18. Bat. Cab. & Term.	—	RE	5.00	2.00
19. Battery.	10.4	S		
20. Starter.	150	S		
21. Gen./Alter.	26	S		
22. Volt. Reg.	13.4	S		
23. Heat Riser.		SE		3.00
24. Brake Fluid.		S		

UNDER CAR INSPECTION   Station II

	Comments	Cond.	Parts	Labor
25. Lights.		S		
26. Seat Belts F R		S		
27. Foot Pedal Adj.		//*		
28. Pkng. Brake Adj.		//*		
29. Toe in Frt. Rear.	6 in.	AJ		
30. Wheel Camber.	−¼ −1	AJ		9.95
31. Wheel Caster.	0 +1½	AJ		
32. Heat Riser.		/*		
33. Eng. Oil Leaks.		S		
34. Freeze Plug Leaks.		S		
35. Trans. Oil Leaks.		S		
36. U-Joint Cond.		S		
37. Diff. & Pinion Leaks.		S		
38. R. Axle Seals.		S		
39. Pipes, Muffler.		S		
40. Brackets, Reson.		S		
41. Fuel L & Hoses.		S		
42. Brake L & Hoses.		S		
43. F. Wheel Bearings.		SE	2.20	NC
44. Drum Cond.	Score	SE		10.00
45. Wheel Cyl. Leaks.	*	R	8.00	10.00
46. Brk. L. Cond.	0 **	RE	24.00	14.50
47. Master Cyl. Leak.		S		

SUSPENSION INSPECTION

	Comments	Cond.	Parts	Labor
48. Strut Bushings.	*	RE	14.00	21.00
49. Idler Arm.	*	RE	13.60	8.50

	Comments	Cond.	Parts	Labor
50. Tie Rods Out.				
Inner.		S		
51. Center Linkage.		S		
52. Ball Joints				
Upper. Lower.		RE	31.30	21.00
53. Control Arm Bushes.		S		
54. Shocks F. R.		S		
55. Tires LF LR RR RF		S		
56. Fr. Wh. Bal. R. L.		SE	1.00	5.00
57. Mtr. or Trans. Mts.		S		

BRAKING EFFICIENCY Station III
OSCILLISCOPE TESTS Station IV

58. Timing at Idle	2½ 3	S		
59. Dist. Mech. Adv.	13½–17½ 16	S		
60. Total Adv.	24 –32½ 31	S		
61. Dist. Cap & Rotor.		S		
62. Coil.		S		
63. Time Pts. Clsd. (dwell)	40–45 40	S		
64. Dist. Wear.		S		
65. Points & Condns.		S		

CARBURETOR TESTS

66. Idle R. P. M.	550	900	AJ		
67. Gulp Valve.			—		
68. A. F. R. Idle (12.4–13)		11	AJ	5.70	
69. A. F. R. Cruise (14–15)		13.8	R		15.00
70. A. F. R. Power (12–13.4)		14.6	R		
71. Acceleration.			S		

LOADED DYNAMOMETER TESTS

72. Trans. Shift Pattern.		S		
73. Drive Train Noise.		S		
74. R. Wheel Bal.		SE		5.00
75. Engine Knocks.		S		
76. Ring Blow-by		S		
77. Oil Consumption		S		
78. Plugs.		SE		
79. % of Cyl. Var.	30%	S		
80. Plug Wire Cond.		S		
81. Speed Accur. 60 mph.	60	S		
82. Overheating		S		

ROAD TEST (OPTIONAL)

	Comments	Cond.	Parts	Labor
83. Trans. Shift Pat.				
84. R. Wheel Bearings				
85. Power Train Noise.				
86. Shock Sway.				
87. Vacuum Modulator.				
Horsepower at 2500 RPM now		44		
Horsepower at 2500 RPM should be		50		

That's an exact copy of the report I was handed by the salesman at the first of the new franchised repair shops that call themselves diagnostic centers.

He gave me a few moments to glance at the report before giving me his pitch.

"This car of yours is in really bad shape," he began. "So bad, in fact, that for your own good I strongly urge you not to drive it home unless you keep your speed down to no more than ten miles an hour."

Like the good salesman he was, he waited for my reaction to his message of foreboding. I told him that I thought the car was running pretty good and that it had never given me any real trouble.

"That just goes to prove how little the average driver knows about the car he drives every day," he stated. "Wear and tear comes on so gradually that you just don't hear the warning sounds or notice the slowly developing loss of efficiency that comes about through everyday usage."

Then he gave me his best shot with his closer. "Here's what I will do for you: if you will agree to have this work done in our shop and leave your car here now, I'll lend you one of our loan cars free of charge and have your car all fixed up and ready for you in two days. Will that be all right?"

He must still remember that nut who got to his feet and replied, "Well, Mr., if you say that I mustn't drive my nice little car at more than ten miles an hour, then ten miles an hour it's going to have to be." With that, I picked up the report and my car keys and left.

Friends, there is just no way a company that depends for the major part of its income on car repairs and tune-ups can ever be relied upon to give you an honest and unbiased report on the condition of your car. Human nature just isn't made that way. That's just the same as asking a restaurant owner whether you look hungry, a barber whether or not you need a haircut, or a furrier whether your wife needs a fur coat. These questions are absolutely rhetorical and lead to the only advice I can give you about the new undersized diagnostic centers. If they have their own repair garage and offer to correct the faults they report on, then avoid them like the plague. It's dollars to donuts that you have discovered just another smart gimmick designed to sell auto repairs.

Take another look at that report with me. This was quite a small garage with very limited facilities. This kind of operation usually does much better if it concentrates on minor repairs and replacements. Usually, the equipment, the tools, and the mechanics are somewhat limited in their scope, and because of this they prefer to avoid engine overhauls and transmission disassembling. Notice, therefore, that although their report sheet lists 87 separate items, all of which are within the capabilities of their service, the report does not include even a simple compression test of the engine. Neither does it make any comment on the condition of the automatic transmission clutches and bands. Search the report thoroughly, as I did, and you will find nothing about the compression values of the engine . . . nothing at all.

Beware of these places. Maybe there are a few that do a good job, and whose lessees are honest men with years of experience and training at their fingertips when they examine your car. But wherever I went during my own check-out of the diagnostic centers, I found no evidence of any altruistic motives behind their operations—only a depressing realization that here was just another smart idea for taking the long-suffering motorist for as much as possible. Even the fee for the report is most unfair. My car was only there for just over one hour, and even in today's inflated hourly labor charges, $18 is, to use Milton's words, "swinish gluttony."

Not wishing to condemn the whole idea unfairly, I took the same car to two other similar operations. One of these charged the same $18 fee, while the other had a special going that week and had reduced their charge to just $12.95. The reports varied only according to the scope of their repair facilities and mechanics' skills. One wanted $286.40 to put my car back in shape, while the other's T. O. man was not so "strong in the box" and only tried for $127.50.

Some weeks after conducting this examination of the diagnostic centers, I was on a promotional tour of the country on behalf of my book, *What You Should Know Before You Buy a Car*. These tours are exciting and do generate a tremendous amount of interest in my writings. Wherever I went, the local car dealers and their associations were waiting to challenge me on television and radio. As you can imagine, some of these debates . . . discussions . . . arguments . . . fights . . . got pretty hairy, but because I only expose the things I know to be true, I have never lost one of these sessions. As a result, I have probably made quite a few enemies in the car business during the past year or two. Would you believe that I have even been banned from appearing at certain television stations, especially those who depend heavily upon the local automobile dealerships for a high percentage of their advertising revenue? On the whole, however, I have been treated extremely generously by the television and radio media, and I would like to give my warmest regards and a tip of the hat to the many great personalities and networks who, without regard to their station's automobile accounts, told me to go ahead and take my best shots.

I was booked to appear on a television talk show in San Diego one morning. It was the usual format, a one-hour show with three guests and the moderator. Now, as a rule on these programs, each guest has a different topic and his specialty is discussed for 15 minutes or so, interspersed with the necessary paid commercials. Without realizing it, the show's producer had booked a man on the same show as myself who had just returned from Washington, where he had been summoned as an expert witness to give evidence before a congressional committee which was at that time investigating the auto repair industry. I had had no idea that he was going to be there, and since this occurred just a few weeks after I had looked into the diagnostic centers, it warmed the cockles of my heart when I heard the moderator promise the viewers that if time permitted he would get the two of us together to discuss the auto repair business during the last few minutes of the show.

During the commercial following his opening announcement, he came over and asked if this would be a good idea. I agreed that it should be quite stimulating, as I wanted to ask a few questions about the new diagnostic centers. The other guest then introduced himself to me and informed me that he was in fact the owner of such a center, and that he hoped I was not going to attack the diagnostic center idea. He then asked me a few questions about my background and the contents of my book, and I followed by asking him a few questions about the auto diagnostic centers. I kept the conversation as brief as he would allow me to, since I prefer always to make my points before the cameras.

Anyway, the next thing I heard was that he had informed the show's moderator that he would not agree to appear with me before the cameras. I was informed that he did not like the questions I had put to him, and that he had not agreed to be on the show in order to be embarrassed by me. The host of the show was quite disgusted, and showed it. Doesn't it give you cause for concern when you hear that a guy like this is called as an expert witness by our legislators, who listen to his recommendations on how to "clean up" the automobile repair business?

During my personal evaluation of the franchised auto diagnostic centers, I collected a great deal of their literature and brochures. I have in my files a report put out by them concerning a test made of 5,003 vehicles chosen at random. According to the report, all of these vehicles were two years old or older. Now that's an odd description of the group of vehicles which was subjected to a test. Does "older" mean that they were 20 years old? Does it mean that most of them were over or under five years old? I've tried to find out more about this test. When and where was it conducted? Who conducted it? Are the records of the test available for inspection? So far, no one seems to want to give me any information about it. So I'll reproduce it here and allow you to judge for yourselves whether or not you believe it to be genuine or whether it is just another sales brochure put out to promote business at the diagnostic centers. Here then, word for word, is the test sheet just as it was handed to me.

An inspection was made, at random, of 5003 vehicles which were two years old or older. The results were startling and should give rise to careful consideration by all car drivers as to the condition of their vehicles. It is with this in mind that we have informed you as to the general condition of your vehicle and what action, if any, you should take to insure your safety, your family's safety, and the safety of all motorists. We are sure that you agree the rapidly rising highway death toll is appalling and is due largely to faulty equipment. The cost of repairs is a small price to pay when compared to injury and death. Below is reprinted the findings of the inspection.

LARGE DIAGNOSTIC LANE SURVEY RESULTS

General	UNSATISFACTORY	
	Number	Percent
Speedometer 45 mph	262	5.23%
Accuracy 60 mph	262	5.23%
Exhaust System Condition	958	19.14%
Oil or Coolant Leaks	2922	58.40%
Headlight Focus/Candle Power	3622	72.39%
Horn	250	4.99%
Windshield Wiper Action	188	3.75%
Crankcase Ventilator Valve	322	6.43%

Just as I did earlier with the report from the diagnostic center, I've used asterisks to indicate figures or statistical conclusions that stagger the imagination and leave me completely baffled.

Directional Signals	557	11.13%
Parking Lights	439	8.77%
Stop-Tail-License Lights	1306	26.10%

TYPE OF TEST	UNSATISFACTORY	
Brakes		
Static Hydraulic Test	228	4.55%
Pedal Reserve	874	17.46%
Parking Brake	760	15.19%
Brake Shoe Action Front	1043	20.84%
Lining Contamination Front	1339	26.76%
Diving Tendency Front	1036	20.70%
Brake Effort Balance Front	1384	27.66%
Brake Shoe Action Rear	830	16.59%
Lining Contamination Rear	866	17.30%
Brake Effort Balance Rear	1188	23.74%
Remove RF LF RR LR	1610	32.18%
Hydraulic Fluid Level	573	11.45%
Hydraulic Fluid Leaks	852	17.02%
Total Cars Tested 5003		

TYPE OF TEST	UNSATISFACTORY	
Suspension-Tires		
Tire Pressure	389	7.77%

Tire Condition	1066	21.30%
Tire Concentricity	754	15.07%
Shock Absorbers RF LF	1709	34.15%
Shock Absorbers RF LF	823	16.45%
Ball Joints	1385	27.68%
Steering Linkage	1105	22.08%
Springs RF LF	34	0.67%
Springs RR LR	158	3.15%
Wheel Balance Front Rear	2323	46.43%
Camber Left	1623	32.44%
Camber Right	1785	35.67%
Caster Left	2633	52.62%
Caster Right	2892	57.80%
Toe-In Ft-Mile	2449	48.95%
Total Cars Tested 5003		

TYPE OF TEST · UNSATISFACTORY

Fuel-System		
Engine Idle Speed	1834	36.65%
Fuel Leaks	262	5.23%
Combustion Idle	1577	31.52%
.... Intermediate	613	12.25%
Efficiency Full Throttle	730	14.59%
Power Enrichment Point	657	13.13%
Manifold Heat Control Valve	1724	34.45%
Throttle Plate Operation	133	2.65%
Choke Operation	997	19.92%
Air Cleaner Restriction	1327	26.52%
Total Cars Tested 5003	9854*	19.69%

TYPE OF TEST · UNSATISFACTORY

Ignition-System		
Basic Timing	2159	43.15%
Total Advance	516	10.31%
Ignition Point Dwell	1809	36.15%
Distributor Wear	164	3.27%
Ignition Coil Output	126	2.51%
Ignition Coil Polarity	39	0.77%
Cap and Rotor	1128	22.54%
Spark Plug Condition	2554	51.04%
Secondary Wiring	832	16.63%
Ignition Point Condition	2488	49.73%
Total Cars Tested 5003	11815*	23.61%

TYPE OF TEST	UNSATISFACTORY	
Lubricants-Coolants		
Anti-Freeze Protection	119	2.37%
Coolant Condition	351	7.01%
Cooling System Condition	366	7.31%
Hoses	1257	25.12%
Fan Belt	1984	39.65%
Water Pump	311	6.21%
Engine Oil Level	1062	21.22%
Transmission Oil Level	257	5.13%
Power Steering Oil Level	240	4.79%
Differential Oil Level	313	6.25%
Total Cars Tested 5003	6260*	12.51%

TYPE OF TEST	UNSATISFACTORY	
Transmission-Clutch		
Trans Shift Point	303	6.05%
Shift Severity	304	6.07%
Auto Trans Oil Analysis	821	16.41%
Clutch Pedal Clearance	224	4.47%
Clutch Condition	68	1.35%
Passing Gear	267	5.33%
Total Cars Tested 5003	1987	6.61%

TYPE OF TEST	UNSATISFACTORY	
Battery-Starter-Gen		
Cables-Case-Cars	2154	43.05%
Cranking Voltage	267	5.33%
Battery Electrical Capacity	237	4.73%
Voltage Regulator	923	18.44%
Gen. Brush Length	293	5.85%
Gen. Bearing Condition	84	1.67%
Starter Solenoid	91	1.81%
General Condition	196	3.91%
Total Cars Tested 5003	4245*	10.60%

TYPE OF TEST	UNSATISFACTORY	
Power Analysis		
Power Test	1211	24.20%
Head Gasket Leak	111	2.21%
Air Cleaner Condition	1574	31.46%
Fuel System Reliability	290	5.79%

Piston Ring Test	474	9.47%
Valve Test	732	14.63%
Driveline Noise & Vibration	993	19.84%
Universal Joints	1147	22.92%
Total Cars Tested 5003	6532*	16.32%

Now, I cannot make heads or tails out of the statistics given in this report, but I have included it in my book because the items listed, as closely as I can remember, are identical with those in the diagnostic check given in Ontario, Canada and are, in my opinion, right in line with what a diagnostic check and report should include. It would be quite funny, if you could disregard the infamy involved; if you compare this list of items checked with the rather sad little elemental report I was handed for my $18, you will find very little similarity.

Before we leave the report on my three-year-old Chevrolet, let me give you a quick breakdown on what they were going to charge me for correcting the deficiencies that they claim to have found. In other words, if I had agreed to let them go ahead and do all of the work they suggested at their stated prices, here is a total of their charges as listed:

Brakes	$ 76.00
Transmission *fluid only* (can you believe?)	23.50
Radiator	35.75
Engine. *Steam clean!!!*	6.00
Carburetor adjustment	22.70
Replace strut bushings and idler arm	112.40
Other required work listed	59.65
Fee for analysis and diagnostic report	18.00
My total repair bill would have been	$354.00

Surely you need no further comment from me about this latest method of giving the American motorist the business.

Diagnostic Centers? I am all for them, and I see no reason why all of our state governments do not start building them today. The cost for each center would compare favorably with the cost of about one mile of highway and could be financed by adding one miserable little cent to the gasoline tax, or by increasing each automobile's road tax tag by $1. The list of benefits to motorists would fill the rest of this book and would be a gigantic step towards cleaning up the automobile repair business in this country. No longer would the service salesman be able to sell service and repairs that are not essential. There would be an immediate reduction in the ridiculous number of deaths and injuries which are a part of the mayhem perpetrated every day on our roads and highways.

With no profit motive involved, any motorist could drive his vehicle into one of these centers and emerge an hour later with an accurate report on the condition of each of the vital components that, if not in good condition, could cost him an expensive repair bill or possibly even the tragedy that can result from a dangerously worn vital part. The motorist would be handed the report on his vehicle without any comment or sales pitch, and unless he was there by order of the police, he could make his own decision about the repairs his car might need. Of course, if the test was ordered by the authorities, then they would make any stipulations considered necessary to protect the rest of us citizens from a dangerously inefficient motor vehicle.

This much I must say. With all of the millions of dollars in tax money that is spent every year on congressional committees to investigate the automobile repair business, to say nothing of the many other millions spent annually in a losing attempt to lower the sickening death and injury rate on our streets and highways, it is high time our legislative representatives sharpened their swords and began cutting into all of the humbug and hypocrisy they know has enveloped every sound proposal for new statutes. Let them for once order the lobbyists to be still.

Let them, on our behalf, demand that real Diagnostic Centers be built, controlled and manned by employees of the state. Let those who make the diagnosis have engineering qualifications that are beyond doubt. Let it become the law that each car licensed by the state must be thoroughly tested at one of these centers, and that its license tag may not be issued until it conforms with the minimum safety standards prescribed by a governing body of automotive engineers.

Road accidents are caused by bad drivers and by bad cars. By taking the simple legislative steps I have proposed, we can be sure that in the years ahead road accidents will only be caused by bad drivers. Then, let us get rid of them too. If things are allowed to go on as they are now, we will all have cause to regret it. *There is nothing in our laws* to prevent anyone with a driver's license from travelling at 65 miles an hour behind you or me in a car that has no brakes at all. *There is nothing in our laws* to prevent that same nut from driving 65 miles an hour on the same road as you or me in a car that has faulty steering gear. *There is nothing in our laws* to prevent another guy from driving 65 miles an hour in the next lane to you or me in a car with suspension so worn out that he cannot keep it in his own lane going around a slight curve in the road. In the time it takes me to type this page, three perfectly innocent people will have been killed and 21 badly injured on the roads of this country because other people are allowed to take badly repaired cars or cars in need of repair into our ever-increasing traffic stream.

What is it going to take for our legislators to get their heads out of the sand? They'll find no answers down there. If their families were slaughtered today by a car with no brakes, would that do it? Don't they realize that bad cars kill more human beings than wars? Maybe, if they ignore me, I will go away. . . .

9

PREVENTION IS BETTER THAN CURE

"An apple a day keeps the doctor away," or so we were assured by our grandparents. But then, of course, they had never heard of the word "smog," which is not only killing a great many of us, in some areas it is also killing a great many apples. In grandma's day, also, we were not exposed to maniacs in overpowered but poorly serviced automobiles hurtling along our highways at more than 60 miles an hour. I believe the current conservative estimate is in excess of 50,000 deaths a year on America's roads. Certainly, it is going to take more than apples to protect us from this style of demise.

You must know among your immediate circle of friends that hale and hearty individual who never seems to get sick, never seems to need any kind of treatment from a doctor, and, after a lifetime of hard work and strenuous living, manages to outlast all of his contemporaries. No doubt he ate his share of apples (apple growers please note), but it would probably also be found that he ate all of the right things, indulged in the right kind of exercise, and made sure that his mental and physical demands for sleep were adequately gratified.

Garage repair bills, just like doctors' bills, can be kept to a minimum if we take reasonably good care of our cars. Little things like nice clean oil, sufficient clean water to drink, nice clean terminals on our batteries, and correct tire pressures all around would prevent at least half of the expensive problems that, when neglected, bring about the kind of car ailments that can only be cured by handing over a good-sized chunk of income to an automobile hospital, which we call a repair garage.

This chapter is not going to lay down any hard and fast rules or make any binding promises, but it will contain information about automotive preventive medicine that many of you may be hearing for the first time, information that, if followed with reasonable regularity, will have the same beneficial effect on your automobile that a good diet, regular exercise, and plenty of sleep have on your physical well-being. These are just a few good ideas that I have found to be effective over the years and that, provided I remember to practice them, keep my cars running reliably and economically.

The subject of oil changes and chassis lubrications is a matter of some confusion for many motorists. The car manufacturers and the oil companies make certain recommendations, but as a result of a cynical attitude inculcated by many years of high-pressure advertising, many motorists are convinced that these exhortations are prompted more by a desire to sell oil than by a genuine interest in the welfare of the customer. Here is my golden rule on this subject. I have my oil changed every 3,000 miles or every two months, whichever comes around first. Let me add that since I adopted this system some 12 years ago, my personal cars have never given me the kinds of trouble that might be caused by insufficient oil changes and lubrications.

By the way, this is one job that I usually have done at my local gas station, and I'll give you two good reasons why I recommend that you do the same. First of all, it is almost always much cheaper than at most new car dealerships. In my area at this time, the new car dealerships are charging $10.50 for an oil change, a chassis lubrication, and a new oil filter cartridge. My local gas station charges just $6.50 for the same service and uses the same brand of motor oil. My second reason for preferring to use the gas station's facilities for this comparatively simple task is that I am able to watch the work being done and can thus be quite sure that every last drip of the sludge that accumulates in an engine's crankcase is allowed to escape before the fresh new oil is poured in. Even at the gas stations, especially if they are busy, you might have to insist that they allow this harmful sludge to drip out for a few minutes longer before they replace the oil plug.

New car dealerships do not, as a rule, permit service customers to stand around in the service stalls and usually usher the customer into some kind of waiting room once the service repair order has been signed. The lube man in almost all new car dealerships is paid so much for an oil change and lube, and if there are other cars waiting, he will understandably try to get as many jobs done in a day as he can. This often results in the oil sump plug being removed just long enough for the quick-running thin oil to run out. As soon as the oil stops running and the damaging sludge begins to drip, the busy operator will often replace the plug and pour in the fresh oil. In my view, this is not an oil change at all. As soon as the engine is restarted, the new oil is immediately mixed with the old abrasive sludge, and this concoction is pumped throughout the engine's oil system, doing as much harm as if the oil had not been changed at all.

It will certainly be to your car's benefit if, no matter where you have your oil changes done, you insist that you be allowed to watch. If the operator starts to replace the oil plug too soon, just tell him to hold off for a few minutes while all the stale old sludge is cleared out of your engine. Certainly there should be at least 20 seconds between each drip before the plug is screwed back in. If you take the time to follow this simple piece of advice, you will add many thousands of miles to the lifespan of your engine and you will almost certainly save hundreds of dollars in ultimate car repair costs or reconditioning charges when the time comes around for that appraiser to value your car at trade-in time. Apart from all of this, clean oil all the way through your engine's circulatory system will cause your engine to perform with a quiet efficiency that will be the envy of your more "know-it-all" friends.

Automatic transmission fluid levels are something else again. My advice is never, never to allow a gas station attendant to make any judgments about your automatic transmission fluid level. There are some who might know what they are doing, but the chances are that most of them will not, and why the heck should it be the motorist who has to take a chance on this kind of well-intentioned but unskilled judgment? Transmission seals are replaced every day as a result of overzealous gas station attendants selling quarts of transmission fluid to motorists whose cars do not need it.

Never take a chance with this costly and vital piece of your car's equipment. Some automatic transmissions give a true level reading only when the selector is in the drive position with the engine running, while others should be in the neutral position. None of them would give the correct reading during the short period the engine is switched off while you stop for gasoline. Just keep this in mind. The purpose of transmission fluid is not primarily to lubricate, as is the case with engine oil; therefore, it is never used up or burned as engine oil always is. As a consequence, unless you find evidence of it leaking on your garage floor, just have it checked once every six months at a new car dealership that specializes in servicing your particular make of car. Perhaps on a cross-country kind of trip you should take a look under your car every morning before moving it from where it has stood overnight. If your transmission has developed a leak, you will find evidence of it on the ground just under where your accelerator pedal is.

If you ever do find evidence of a transmission leak, no matter how small, do not delay. Drive straight to the nearest new car dealership that handles your make of car and have it checked out. You might well save yourself a transmission repair bill amounting to over $200.

But please, *never allow a gas station attendant to sell you transmission fluid.* If he comes around to your window and tells you that you need a quart or two of fluid, first get out of the car and look underneath it to see if your transmission is leaking. If it is not, then thank him for his trouble and drive to the nearest dealership and have them check it for you.

This chapter is not a course in automobile engineering, by any means. Learning how to apply a Band-aid or when to take an aspirin doesn't mean you're aspiring to become a doctor. It s my belief that motorists as a rule simply neglect to apply the Band-aid or take the aspirin that might quickly clear up the minor ailments to which all automobiles are prone and which, if neglected in their early stages, will inevitably lead to painfully expensive treatment at one of the automobile "hospitals." If you will just take a few minutes every month to check out one or two very simple items on your car, I promise that you will save a great deal of money and inconvenience during the years ahead. If every motorist would take this advice, the $25 billion that we now spend every year in this country on automobile repairs would be cut by at least half.

Things like belts. Yes, just plain, everyday 50¢ belts. You know that they're there under the hood of your car, because you've seen them there whenever you've raised the hood. Tell the truth now, are you sure that the belts on your car are in good condition, that they are tight enough, and that they are not slipping? Considering the great stresses and heat that these little drive belts are subjected to every day, they stand up to their task extremely well, but they do gradually stretch; and for this reason, the manufacturers always design their engines so that the belts can be tightened easily and in just a couple of minutes by moving whatever the drive pulley is attached to.

Today's automobiles contain more enjoyable luxuries than most homes, items like air conditioning, AM and FM multiplex stereo, power windows, power seats, power trunk locks, power steering, power brakes, power door locks, and even electric shavers. Every year, something new is added to make your motoring more enjoyable and convenient. But have you ever stopped to realize that none of these things works independently, that they must all be hooked on to your car's already overtaxed engine and power system, and that as each item comes into use a greater and greater strain is placed on those little belts that transmit the power from your engine to the generator, the air conditioning, the power steering, and the rest? Why, it's even a little belt that drives the fan that cools the radiator. If a belt becomes slack or so smooth that it slips on the pulley, the fan will slow down and your engine will overheat, the generator or alternator will not recharge the battery enough to replace the electricity that all of those nice luxury items use up, and as a result of just these two things your overheated engine will run badly and you'll find yourself one morning with a dead battery. All of this trouble caused by belts, plain old 50¢ belts.

Here's a little job that you can have attended to without charge any time you stop for gasoline. When the attendant asks if you would like him to check under the hood, tell him not to bother checking your transmission fluid level, but that you would appreciate it if he would check to see if your belts are tight enough and in good condition. Most gas stations keep a good stock of drive belts around in all sizes, and they will fit a new one on any car for very little money. I know of few things more important to the efficient running of today's automobile than these little drive belts, and I strongly urge you to make sure that they are tight enough and strong enough to do their important job efficiently.

One warning here. *Never* . . . that's *never ever*, put your hand anywhere near these belts while the engine is running. They are exposed, and they transmit enormous power from the engine. *Any* carelessness in this area can result in a terrible accident. People have had their hands torn off by allowing them to be caught in these belts. Make it a rule now that you will not touch them at any time, but do remember to ask the man at the gas station to check them for tightness and strength every time you fill your gas tank.

Here now are a few helpful hints about your car. There are certain warning sounds that come from automobiles, and if you recognize and act upon them as soon as possible, you will prevent considerable inconvenience and sometimes forestall an expensive replacement.

If you notice that there is a sharp "tap, tap," coming from under the hood of your car when the engine is running poorly and idling unevenly, it may be that one of the spark plugs is not properly insulated, causing the spark to jump from the plug to ground itself on the engine block. This is more likely to occur in wet weather or a damp atmosphere and can be corrected while you wait by any mechanic. The same problem could be caused by one of the spark plug wires detaching itself from the top of the spark plug. It will cause your engine to idle very badly and may give you cause for great concern. However, provided that you recognize the symptom I have just described, and provided you don't run into a mechanic looking for a big job like a major tune-up, as soon as he pushes the plug wire back onto the plug your car should immediately regain its reassuring surge of power.

If you begin to notice that your engine is sounding more

like an entry in the Indianapolis 500 and gives a throaty roar whenever you press the accelerator, either you have developed a hole in the muffler, or the exhaust pipe leading from the exhaust manifold to the muffler is worn out or has become disconnected from the mufflerbox. It might be a good idea, when you stop by a repair garage to have this seen to and when they raise your car up on the hoist, for you to walk underneath it with the mechanic and have him show you what is wrong. They just *might* try to sell you a new muffler and complete exhaust system when your trouble could be cured by replacing just one section of pipe.

A loud squeal whenever you apply your brakes does not automatically mean that your brake linings are worn out. Sometimes a little condensation in the brake drums will cause them to squeak for a while, especially first thing in the morning or after your car has stood parked for a long time. In areas where there is a lot of rain and dampness, this is a common problem. However, if the squeals persist throughout the day, have your brakes checked as soon as possible. The squeals are the first warning symptom that your metal brake lining shoes are touching the brake drum itself, and unless new fiber-covered brake shoes are installed straightaway, the unprotected shoes will cut a deep score mark in the drums and necessitate the costly job of having the drums removed and refaced on a turning lathe.

Strange sounds coming from the engine give most automobile owners palpitations, especially if they have never learned how to recognize one sound from another. As a general rule, an uncommon sound coming from the engine that is not accompanied by a noticeable change in the performance and efficiency of the car can be corrected quickly and will not cost you an arm and a leg. The most common of these is probably the sticking valve lifter. This is a kind of muffled clicking or tapping sound which will speed up as the engine speed is increased and slow down to a click every second or two when the engine is just idling. If this happens to your car, first check to be sure that your engine is not overdue for an oil change. If you find the oil to be clean and up to the correct level on your dip stick, you might try having your gas station man add a quart of upper cylinder lubricant to your oil while the engine is running, and then see if the sound disappears after a further 50 or 60 miles of driving. If this fails, then you should take your car to your favorite mechanic and have him remove the valve cover and check to see if the small and very narrow oil pipe that keeps the valve lifters lubricated has become blocked. Valve lifters very rarely lose their original adjustment and should never be tightened or loosened before all of the checks I have suggested have first been tried.

Another unusual sound you might hear occasionally from your car's engine compartment as you drive along is something like the last of the bath water disappearing down the drain, a prolonged rattling sound that occurs only as you accelerate. In 99 cases out of 100, this simply means that the gas station attendant has pumped regular gasoline into your tank instead of the higher octane premium (assuming your engine is a high-compression V8 type); or it could be caused by stale gasoline being pumped in. This sometimes happens when you stop for gas at a station situated off the beaten track, where the gasoline has stood for too long in their tanks.

You will recall from an earlier chapter my comments on the stale gasoline that is sometimes purchased by some independent gas stations. If you suddenly notice the bath water sound, try to recall if you have stopped recently at any of these stations, and if you have, then just put up with the strange sound until you use up all of the gasoline in your tank. Do not buy any more until your gas gauge indicates that your tank is almost empty, then fill it up with any premium brand of high octane gasoline. The nasty rattling bath water should then disappear, and your trouble should be at an end. If this doesn't do the trick, then you are going to need the services of a mechanic to advance the spark timing; this shouldn't cost more than a few dollars, providing that nothing more serious is involved.

There is another sound similar to the last one, except that it is a little harsher and more like metal on metal. This could be your heat riser giving you trouble, and you should have this seen to as soon as possible, since neglect in this case could mean the difference between a small job and a small bill and the other kind nobody enjoys except the garage cash register.

If you ever hear a high-toned whistle followed by an occasional rumbling sound coming from up front as you come to a stop after a long drive, you have an overheated engine. It's dollars to donuts either that you have a broken or a too-slack fan belt, or that your radiator is just about out of water. Get your car to the nearest gas station, provided there is one within a block or so. If you are some distance from the nearest station, then pull your car over to the side of the road and switch the engine off. Raise the hood so that as much cooler air as possible can get to your engine, and do not, repeat, *do not* touch anything. Do not attempt to restart the car for at least 45 minutes, but spend that time trying to beg, borrow, or steal some clean water for your radiator.

After 45 minutes, standing back as far as you can, reach out and, with a handkerchief or a piece of rag, slowly slacken off your radiator cap. If steam starts to rush out, do not be alarmed. Just let go of the cap and leave it where it is until all of the steam pressure has escaped. Then it will be quite safe to unscrew the cap the rest of the way and remove it. If you can get hold of enough water to fill the radiator, so much the better. If not, pour in all that you can get, replace the cap tightly, and, with the hood still up, get in and restart your engine. Before closing down the hood, take a look at the fan to see if it is running. If it is not, then that gas station had better not be more than four or five minutes driving time away, or you'll probably do severe damage to your car. If you have any doubts, don't take a chance; find a telephone and call a garage for help.

If your car has power steering and starts to chirp and gabble like a soprano turkey when you turn your steering wheel, more noticeably when maneuvering the car at slow speed, this almost surely means that the belt that drives the power steering unit is slipping. Never attempt to adjust this yourself. Your mechanic can do it quickly and correctly in just a couple of minutes. You might also have him check the level in your power steering fluid cup. If this is not up to the mark specified by the manufacturer, your power steering action will become "lumpy" and jerky.

Another bird-like sound coming from underneath the car would probably be caused by a rear axle pinion bearing seal getting too dry. If you have it seen to right away, it's not much of a job, and the birds will sing somewhere else. Don't leave this for too long, however, or it will cost you real money to fix.

If your car develops a faint but constant whine, you've more than likely got a worn wheel bearing. You cannot fix this once the whine starts, so let your mechanic replace the bearing for you.

A louder whine which only sounds off when you are either slowing down or coasting is usually bad news. It indicates that you have trouble with your rear axle gears or differential, and this almost always means replacing some costly parts and a fairly high labor charge.

Shock absorbers wear out in time and should be replaced as soon as possible after you hear a clanking, bell-like sound coming from under the car. Sometimes replacing just the worn bushings will do the trick, and this should not be too costly.

For a few years now, new cars have been blessed with alternators instead of generators by the manufacturers. In many ways the alternator is an improvement. For one thing, you cannot overtax the battery no matter how much of your electrical equipment you use at the same time. Just so long as you keep your engine running, even if only idling, your alternator will replace all of the electrical charge you use up. There's just one thing that an alternator will not do, however, and ignorance of this one drawback will often give the unknowing motorist one big problem. An alternator will not charge a car battery at all.

Get this straight now: it will replace all the electricity your car uses, *provided that you keep the engine running.* If you park with your best girl for a few hours and listen to the radio, or leave your car for a lengthy period at night and forget to turn off the headlights, your battery may well run down. Even though the car may start all right, no matter how long the journey home, your alternator will not recharge your battery on the way. My advice is to have your battery charged up at your local gas station once every year, more often if you make a habit of listening to the radio down lovers' lane.

Some of you have no doubt taken delivery of a brand new car and within a day or two have come up with a flat battery. This simply means that the battery was not fully charged when you took delivery of the car. Cars that have been on display in a new car dealer's showroom are especially prone to this problem for their eventual new owner. People get in and out of new cars on display all day long and are constantly turning on and off much of the car's electrical equipment while the engine stands dormant. As a consequence, there is sometimes only enough charge left to start the car when the customer picks it up, and since the alternator will not charge the battery up, the battery is in the same uncharged condition when he gets his new car home as it was when he took delivery.

As this chapter's title indicates, I am passing on some of the simpler things that almost any motorist can do to forestall an expensive repair and to keep his car in peak condition.

Whenever you take the time and trouble to check out the little items I have suggested, you are keeping your car one step further away from the repair shop and adding to your family's enjoyment and safety.

Here's something else you might watch out for. Do not confuse a wheel alignment with a wheel balance. A wheel balance is a small task and quite inexpensive, whereas a wheel alignment properly done can be quite expensive. Your car needs a wheel alignment when your tires show unusual wear on one edge of the tread or give evidence of any uneven tread wear. When your tires seem to thump on the road as you travel along, then it's almost certain that your wheels need balancing. Have your wheels balanced twice a year. For this small expense, you can expect longer tire life, safer braking, and a much smoother ride, and since your unbalanced wheels will not be shaking your front end out of line, you will ultimately save money on less frequent front end alignments.

There's something else that you may want to try. The next time your car begins to idle poorly and starts giving bad gas mileage and poor acceleration, go out to it one dark evening when it is sitting in your garage or carport. Keeping all the lights out in the garage or carport, raise the hood and then get in and start the engine. In that pitch blackness, stand for a while and watch under the hood. Many ignition faults or leaks can be detected in this way. You'll be looking for little blue sparks or a blue glow around any electrical part. By detecting faulty ignition wiring, a crack in your distributor cap, spark plug cables that need replacing, or possibly a coil cap with a bad connection, you might well be able to diagnose your own problem and avoid having to pay between $50 and $75 for a major tune-up. Just think how respectful your mechanic is going to be when you tell him just to replace a particular spark plug cable or the plastic distributor cap. Try it once; you might find it quite interesting, and certainly it will save you some money in the long run.

There is, of course, a great deal more to learn about automobiles, but I think you now know enough to get yourself out of most minor troubles. Keep this book around somewhere handy, just in case your car starts to act up one of these days. If you can't find the answer to your problem from it right away, try giving the plastic case covering your voltage regulator a sharp blow with the edge of the book, and then try starting your car again. If that doesn't do the trick, then perhaps you'd better call your garage—just so long as you don't say to the guy who answers the phone, "Something seems to be wrong with my car . . . and I think I've run the battery down."

10

HOW GOOD IS YOUR 5 YEAR-50,000 MILE NEW CAR WARRANTY?

The new car salesman was rather vague about it, but he did assure you that your new car purchase was protected by the manufacturer's warranty for a period of five years or 50,000 miles, whichever came first. He probably made it one of his main selling points before closing the deal with you, and let's face it, you were more than impressed by the salesman's comforting assurance that the manufacturer would pick up the entire tab, should anything mechanical go wrong with the car.

You were probably not allowed to read the terms of the warranty before you signed up for the deal. It's just as likely that even when you picked up the new car you were told that the warranty card had to be registered in your name, that it would be a few days before it would be ready for you. Am I right so far? Let us see if I can be right for a little while longer. When you finally had the warranty card in your possession, you did *not* take the time to read and understand its terms and conditions. Right? Only later, when you had your first sign of trouble with the car and you took it in for some repairs or service, were you finally brought down to earth by a sizable repair bill for the items or type of service not covered by the manufacturer's new car warranty.

The automobile business seems to be determined to mislead and infuriate its customers. It has been my experience that even when it has nothing to lose by being straight and honest in its approach, there is a reluctance to set the customer straight and allow him to clearly understand the situation. One of these days, I expect to be in a new car dealership and find that the door marked EXIT will lead me into the men's washroom.

Most of you take delivery of your new car without fully understanding the terms and conditions of your new car warranty, so here, once and for all, we are going to clearly explain it's advantages and it's limitations. Let us take the New Vehicle Warranty for 1970 of one of the top 3 manufacturers and go through it carefully together. If you happen to be the owner of a new Chevrolet, Ford, or Chrysler product, it will make little or no difference; these paragons of the competitive free enterprise system just happen to issue new car warranties which are as closely aligned as their suggested new car prices. In other words, if you've seen one you've seen them all.

——— NEW VEHICLE WARRANTY

——— warrants to the original retail purchaser that it will repair or replace, at it's option, any parts of each new 1970 ——— passenger car vehicle and chassis (referred to as "Vehicle"), including all equipment and accessories thereon (except tires) manufactured or supplied by ———, which are returned to an authorized ——— dealer at his place of business and which examination discloses to ——— reasonable satisfaction to be defective in material or workmanship under normal use and service. Such repairs and replacements shall be performed by such dealer without charge.

This Warranty is subject to the following provisions:

LIMITATIONS

12 Month-12,000 Mile Coverage

This Warranty applies to the entire vehicle (except tires) for 12 months from the date of delivery to the original retail purchaser or until the vehicle has been driven for 12,000 miles, whichever first occurs.

5 Year-50,000 Mile Coverage

Upon expiration of the 12 month-12,000 mile Warranty coverage, this Warranty continues to apply to the vehicle's power train components until the expiration of five years from the date of delivery to the original retail purchaser or until it has been driven for 50,000 miles, whichever first occurs. Vehicle's power train components are:

* cylinder block, head, all internal engine parts, water pump, and intake manifold;
* transmission case and all internal transmission parts including torque converter;
* propeller shaft and universal joints; and
* drive axle, differential, and axle shafts.

If, at the time of delivery to the original retail purchaser, the vehicle has been in factory or dealer service (as a demonstrator, for example) the time and mileage limitations shall be calculated from the date the vehicle was first placed in such factory or dealer service.

EXCLUSIONS

This Warranty shall not apply to:

1. Normal maintenance services (such as engine tune-up, fuel system cleaning, carbon or sludge removal, brake and clutch adjustments, and wheel alignment and balancing):
2. The replacement of service items (such as spark plugs, ignition points, positive crankcase ventilator valves, filters

and brake and clutch linings) made in connection with normal maintenance services;

3. Normal deterioration of soft trim and external appearance items due to wear and exposure;

4. The repair or replacement of any part, the failure of which is caused by lack of performance of required maintenance as specified by —————— in the "1970 New Vehicle Warranty and Owner Protection Plan" folder attached;

5. Any part of a vehicle which has been subject to misuse, negligence, alteration or accident so as in any way, in the reasonable judgement of ——————, to affect adversely its performance and reliability;

6. Any vehicle on which the odometer mileage has been altered and the vehicle's actual mileage cannot be readily determined;

7. Any vehicle for which the owner does not possess a —————— Protect-O-Plate issued in the owner's name; or

8. Any vehicle registered and normally operated outside the United States or Canada (the Warranty applicable to such Vehicle shall be that authorized by —————— in the country where such vehicle is registered and normally operated).

Sole Warranty

This Warranty is the only Warranty, expressed or implied, applicable to the Vehicle. —————— neither assumes nor authorizes any other person to assume for it any other obligation or liability in connection with the Vehicle.

Owner Responsibility

1. REQUIRED MAINTENANCE SCHEDULE

As an express condition of the —————— New Vehicle Warranty, the following maintenance operations are to be per-

formed at the specified intervals by an authorized —————
dealer or any service station or garage regularly providing
such services: ENGINE OIL—Change every four months
or 6,000 miles, whichever occurs first, or every two months
or 3,000 miles under certain operating conditions. (See
Owner's Manual.)

OIL FILTER—Replace at first oil change and every second
oil change thereafter.

CHASSIS LUBRICATION—Lubricate suspension every 4
months or 6,000 miles, whichever first occurs. Maintain all
oil and fluid levels.

CARBURETOR AIR CLEANER—Inspect every 12,000
miles, replace if necessary. Replace at least every 24,000
miles. Inspect and replace more frequently under dusty operating conditions.

POSITIVE CRANKCASE VENTILATION VALVE—Re-
place each 12 months or 12,000 miles, whichever first occurs.

AUTOMATIC TRANSMISSION SERVICE—Drain and replenish fluid every 24,000 miles, or every 12,000 miles under
severe operating conditions. (See Owner's Manual.) Adjust
Powerglide low band at first fluid change. Replace Turbo
Hydra-matic sump strainer at 24,000 miles.

ENGINE COOLANT—Drain and replenish every two years.
Refer to your 1970 Owner's Manual for further information
on vehicle maintenance.

2. OWNER'S MANUAL

*We urge you to read the 1970 ————— OWNER'S MANUAL
carefully* and follow the recommendations therein to help assure enjoyable and satisfactory operation of your Vehicle.
Proper maintenance and care of the Vehicle will help you
achieve lower over-all operating costs. Also, regular and
proper maintenance of the Vehicle by competent technicians
will help you avoid conditions arising from negligence which
are not covered by the ————— New Vehicle Warranty.

Delco Energizer (Battery)

The Energizer in your Vehicle is warranted against defects in material and workmanship under the terms of the ———— New Vehicle Warranty for a period of twelve (12) months from the date of delivery to the original retail purchaser (or date of service if the Vehicle was previously in dealer or factory service) or until it is driven for 12,000 miles, whichever first occurs. Replacement of the Energizer, in the event of any such defect during this warranty period, will be made at no charge. In addition to the warranty coverage, the Delco Energizer is covered for an Adjusted Service Period commencing with the expiration of the 12-month or 12,000-mile portion of the New Vehicle Warranty and expiring thirty-six (36) months from the date of delivery to the original retail purchaser, or date of initial service, whichever first occurs.

Should the Energizer in your Vehicle prove defective under normal passenger car use within the Adjusted Service Period, the defective Energizer can be replaced on a pro-rata adjustment basis which provides you with a credit toward the purchase of a new Energizer of equal or greater capacity based on the number of months remaining in the Adjusted Service Period at the time the Energizer is found defective. Contact an authorized ———— or Energizer Dealer for further information on warranty adjustments during the Adjusted Service Period.

The provisions of these Energizer Service Adjustments shall not apply (A) to failure in service due to misuse, negligence or accident, including but not limited to improper installation, freezing, failure to have Energizer inspected regularly and filled with colorless, odorless drinking water when needed, use of electrolyte other than "battery grade" sulphuric acid solution of a specific gravity recommended by

————, or (B) to costs for recharging this Energizer or for the use of a rental Energizer.

There it is then, your 1970 New Car Warranty. Those of you who didn't bother to read and understand the copy which came with your new car, probably didn't bother to read this copy either. You are the ones I hear creating a disturbance in the service department at the dealership with which I am associated, when the service manager insists that the factory warranty does not include front end alignments or wheel balancing. You come in with your car and sign the repair order instructing the work to be done. Then, later in the day, you almost burst a blood vessel when you are quite properly billed for all of the work the factory will not compensate the dealership for. For goodness sake, stop right here and go back a couple of pages and carefully read the terms of a new car warranty. If you cannot be bothered to do this, then this chapter (and probably this whole book) is going to leave you as uninformed as you were before you started reading it.

Probably the most important reason for knowing the limitations of your new car warranty before you take delivery of your new car is that if the car has not been properly prepared and serviced for you before you drive it home, you are almost certainly going to have to pay to have those items corrected when you bring the car back, even if it's only a day later. Most dealerships protect themselves from any liability by having each customer sign a statement acknowledging satisfaction with the condition of the car at the time of delivery. Once they have this agreement, signed by the new owner, in their possession, they are perfectly within their rights, and are conforming to the terms of the new car warranty, to charge for any kind of work not covered by the manufacturer's liability.

Item: *never sign the delivery satisfaction sheet or take*

delivery of your new car before checking out this item very carefully. Front end wheel alignment and wheel balancing are not covered by the manufacturer's warranty, neither are they even on the list of things included in the manufacturer's recommended new car dealer preparation. When I first ran into this kind of beef from a customer, I asked the factory representative why in heaven's name neither of these important items were included in the dealer's list of items to be taken care of during the new car preparation. He informed me that this work was done at the factory and that therefore, when a customer brings the car back for a wheel alignment, he must have banged the wheel against the curb a couple of times since taking delivery.

My sympathy here is with the complaining customer, and anyone who has watched new cars being loaded on or unloaded from transporter trucks would have to agree. It would not be possible to devise a more efficient manner of throwing a vehicle's front end out of alignment than to drive and bump it along narrow steel channels like those on the transporters. Since all new cars reach the dealerships on these special trucks, service garages and front end alignment technicians are assured of millions of dollars in extra income every year. It has been my experience that far too many new cars are delivered to the buyers with their front end out of alignment and my readers should make a point of insisting that wherever they buy that new car, it be agreed in writing on their copy of the deal and signed by the manager, that a front end alignment will be done on the car at the dealership before delivery.

Getting back to the new car warranty again, you will find that the 5 Year-50,000 mile coverage is limited and includes only the engine's cylinder block, cylinder head, and the internal engine parts. Notice please, that it does *not* include the carburetor or any part of the car's ignition system, the distributor, the coil, the starter motor, the starter solenoid switch, the voltage regulator, the generator or any of the wiring system. It *does* include the water pump, the intake manifold, the transmission case, and all internal transmission parts including the torque converter. It does *not* include the transmission linkage, the fuel pump, the cooling system, the radiator, the lighting system, the windshield wiper motors, the power steering, the power brakes, the power seats, the power windows, the steering system, the wheels, the suspension system, the shock absorbers, the wheel bearings, the brake cylinders, or the door locks. It *does* include the propeller shaft, the drive axle, the axle shafts, the universal joints, and the differential gears, but it does *not* include the tie rods, the strut rods, the exhaust system, and the mufflers.

So you see, the salesman's vague but rather all-encompassing gesture used to describe the five year warranty at the time he sold you the car was somewhat misleading. Right? It is little wonder that there are angry confrontations between the customer and the service manager, especially in those cases where the customer did not bother to read and understand his new car warranty fully and brought his car in for warranty work with 13,000 miles on the odometer, only to be informed that the warranty period on that particular part expired at 12,000 miles.

Do not accept the salesman's assurance that your new car is diligently worked on before delivery to you. Some dealerships do a very fine job in this regard, but I'm afraid far too many of them just do enough to make sure that the car will drive away from the dealer's premises. They have no difficulty persuading the new car buyer to accept the car even when everything isn't running as well as he would have liked. After all, that nice 5 Year-50,000 Mile Warranty covering both parts and labor will take care of everything in time. Right? That's what he thinks! After all, he didn't insist on examining a copy of the warranty when he made the deal. He inferred more than was implied when the salesman described the warranty in glowing terms. If he's dumb enough not to demand to read the warranty, he's dumb enough to accept delivery of a new car with little more new car preparation than can be purchased for $1 at the local car wash. Once again, many dealerships do a pretty good job on new car preparation, but we are not concerned with these. It's the others, the mean ones, that I want you to know more about. The places where they would rather spend the new car preparation money on television commercials than on an hour or 2 of work, making sure their customer is getting good value.

Once you have been sucked in by one of these hard-nosed organizations, you are almost certainly going to have some problems. Even if you bring the car back the very next day, you will be asked to pay for any work they do on items not covered by the manufacturer's warranty, things like tune-up, fuel system cleaning, brake adjustments, clutch adjustments, transmission adjustments, wheel balancing, front end alignment, spark plugs, ignition points, PCV smog valves, oil filters, air filters, fuel filters, paint scratches or blemishes, any faults in the chrome fittings including the bumpers, door handles, front grille and window surrounds, any tears in the seating, headlining or interior trim and even the glass windshield and windows in the car. These items are not clearly covered under the terms of the manufacturer's warranty and the kind of dealership which did not bother to take care of them during the new car's preparation, will almost surely contest any claims you care to make under the terms of your warranty. It is possible that by going to the trouble and expense of retaining a decent attorney, you might eventually win a court decision directing the dealership to correct certain of these items. You'll almost certainly discover by the time you win your case, however, that it would have been cheaper and less frustrating to have swallowed your fury and chagrin as soon as you discovered that you had been plucked, and paid to have your problems taken care of correctly at a more reputable dealership.

I cannot stress this too strongly: you should never take delivery of a new car before you check it out carefully, preferably with a knowledgeable friend along to give you moral support and informed advice. If you find that the car is not in satisfactory condition in every way, *do not* take delivery of it with just the verbal assurance from the salesman or manager that the offending items will be "taken care of" the following day or when you bring it in for the 1,000 miles service. The only way for you to go is to either refuse to take delivery of the car until the work has been completed, or to insist on a statement on the company's letter head and dated, undertaking to have the repairs, adjustments or replacements done at no expense to you, within a stated time period. This undertaking must be signed by the manager of the dealership (certainly not by a salesman). If it were my car, I would also have it in writing that a current model car be placed at my disposal without charge during the time my car was in their service department for the work to be done. Without such a signed undertaking, I would not accept delivery of the car no matter what kind of blandishments were used to persuade me. Just remember that a car is not sold until the buyer accepts delivery of it, but once you drive it away from the dealership with the documents all signed, you haven't a legal leg to stand on.

There is no valid reason why your new car should not be delivered to you in first class running order and looking and acting in every way like a brand new automobile. Anything less than this would indicate that the dealership is more interested in taking your money than it is in pleasing you as a valued customer. You will notice that there will be nothing overlooked or careless about their attitude when it comes to getting all of the paperwork and legal documents signed in the right places by you before you get your hands on the new car. They will not shrug their shoulders when it comes to the conditional sales contract and tell you that you can take care of that when you bring the car in for the 1,000 miles service. You have the right to expect that they show at least the same amount of interest in your side of the deal and if they do not, then you are entitled to express your suspicions and your annoyance by insisting that their promises be given to you in writing and *signed by the manager or the dealer himself.*

It is my opinion that much of the manufacturer's New Car Warranty is worded in terms that are insufficiently definitive. Many of the items are left to the discretion of either the dealership's service manager or the manufacturer's representative. As there are many thousands of service managers and many hundreds of manufacturer's representatives, the rather insignificent new car buyer is forced to depend on the whims and judgements of these individuals, rather than knowing for sure where the warranty begins and where it ends as far as his particular car is concerned. It is to be hoped that this chapter will encourage my readers to adjust their attitudes toward the new car warranties which come with their new car purchases.

Do not expect to be welcomed with open arms and a generous attitude when you take your car in for work which you believe is covered by your warranty. In some dealerships, you will be treated quite well, but in far too many, you will find that the vague terms of the warranty will allow the discretion of the service manager to decide whether or not you will have to pay for the repairs your car needs.

Give yourself an edge right at the outset, by insisting the new car be in near perfect condition *before* you agree to take delivery and remember that a dealership which would attempt to persuade a customer to take delivery of a new car that had not been carefully and efficiently serviced before delivery would almost certainly be difficult to deal with later, when you bring the car back to have these preparation inadequacies taken care of.

We have so far covered the manufacturer's and the dealership's liability regarding your new car warranty. There is, of course, another side to this agreement which comes under the heading of Owner Responsibility. Let us now examine this important clause in the manufacturer's undertaking to their customers. Everything we are going to check out is in writing on the warranty certificate, but for those among you who didn't bother to read the warranty when you received it, and for those who read it but didn't bother to fully absorb all of it's implications, we will go through it carefully together once and for all.

If you refer back to the items under Required Maintenance Schedule in the new car warranty, you will see that in order to maintain the warranty coverage, you are required to have the engine oil changed either every *four months* or every *6,000 miles*, whichever comes around first. Now this does appear to be quite reasonable, but be careful unless you drive your car more than 18,000 miles every year. Most people who read this condition of their new car warranty, seem to remember only the 6,000 miles, the 4 months time limit just doesn't seem to register with most new car owners for longer than it takes them to read the terms of the warranty. More than half of the cars in this country are driven less than 12,000 miles a year, so if you are one of these owners and you have your oil changed after each 6,000 miles, your new car warranty has been invalidated legally just 4 months after you buy the car. Many dealerships will object to my pointing this out to you, and they will insist that they would still honor the warranty under these circumstances. Maybe they would (at least some of them), but maybe there are those who are delighted to find any reason to charge a service customer as often as they legally can.

Just ask yourself right now, have you been having that

new car's oil changed every 4 months? Notice also in the very next sentence that "under certain operating conditions" the oil must be changed no later than every *3,000 miles* or every *two months*. That's very often and it forces the unfortunate new car buyer once again to be at the tender mercies of either the dealership's service manager or the factory service representative. Maybe the reason why the mileage limitation registers in the average person's mind because they print the figure in numbers, 6,000 miles or 3,000 miles, whereas the time allowance is printed in words like "four months" or "two months." I'm sure it would register more completely with most people if figures were used all the way through the warranty, so that this clause would read 4 months or 2 months.

Check this out thoroughly now in your own mind and make sure that you are following the rules laid down by the manufacturer in your warranty. Just by following this one piece of advice, you might save yourself a whole lot of grief, to say nothing of the money, if and when you need to make a claim under the terms of your new car's warranty.

The next clause after the rule concerning oil changes requires you to have your engine's oil filter replaced at the first oil change and every second oil change thereafter. Now that's a lot of oil filters and remember that you pay for the oil filters. If you didn't thoroughly absorb this short sentence in your warranty certificate, you're probably already in trouble. From this moment on, please ask the man to replace your oil filter every second time you have the oil changed.

The next 2 items listed under Owner Responsibility are Chassis Lubrication and Carburetor Air Cleaner. I can find nothing in either of these requirements that should give you any problems. Just remember to have your chassis lubricated each time you have the oil changed. The correct way to instruct the service writer when you take your car in for this work is to say, "I want an oil change and lubrication and will you please check all of the fluid levels." All of this work is done by the same operator in the lube rack and provided you instruct him to do so, he will check and where necessary, top up the fluid levels in your car's transmission, brake system, power steering hydraulic system and the cooling system. Some garages include all of this automatically whenever they give a car an oil change and lubrication, but it's just as well to have a record of the work being done on your copy of the repair order, just in case you need to prove your compliance with the terms of the warranty at some later date. Some lube men will always be trying to beat the flat rate. By skipping the fluid levels on a few cars every day, they are able to ticket many more repair orders before pay day comes around.

With regard to the carburetor air cleaner, you will recall my remarks about this important but often neglected piece of equipment in an earlier chapter. Personally, I believe in having the air cleaner cleaned or replaced more frequently than the manufacturers require under the terms of their warranty. Much depends, of course, on the atmosphere in your particular locale, but you should remember that your engine needs about 15 times the amount of good clean air as it does gasoline vapor in order to give it's best performance for you. A dirty carburetor air cleaner element makes it next to impossible for any air to get into the carburetor. Keep it clean and you will save a lot of money and enjoy a much better running automobile.

The next item on the list of owner's required maintenance schedule is our old friend, the positive crankcase ventilation valve. This item has infuriated me ever since it first became mandatory in my home state of California. I think it was back in 1960 or 1961 when some well-intentioned but uninformed person in high office decided that this simple little non-return valve would end our smog problems. Here we are some 10 years later and the smog outside my window prevents me from enjoying even the outline of the beautiful Hollywood

Hills which reach up through the smog layer just a short distance away. By law you must have one on your car. The car manufacturers insist, under the terms of their new car warranties, that you have the darned thing replaced every 12,000 miles or every 12 months, whichever comes around first—you'd better remember to have this done if you want to keep your warranty in good standing.

AUTOMATIC TRANSMISSION SERVICE REQUIREMENTS

Watch out here. The warranty reads, "drain and replenish fluid every 24,000 miles, or every 12,000 miles under severe operating conditions." You would be wise to have a little talk with the service manager at the dealership where you bought your new car in order that you may know, before any transmission troubles come, whether your idea of severe operating conditions and his are about the same. Here again, when a warranty claim is made, the decision is left to the service manager and the factory service representative, whether or not your warranty claim will be allowed. Don't wait until something goes wrong to find out about this. Transmission overhauls or replacements are very expensive and more than aggravating, especially when they are needed on a car with only 20,000 miles showing on the odometer. The comforting assurance of a 5 Year-50,000 Mile Warranty disappears in a hurry when a demand for 2 or 3 hundred dollars is thrust in front of you. It costs you nothing to establish a mutual understanding on these matters with your service manager, so for goodness sake take care of this right away, if you haven't already done so.

There is a separate and quite lengthy section in your new car warranty regarding the battery which comes with your car. I feel that I can add a little to the manufacturer's words, and by doing so, perhaps save you some money and certainly a considerable amount of annoyance and inconvenience.

The batteries on today's new cars do a great deal of work for us. When you consider all of the new comforts and luxuries that we enjoy (air conditioning, power windows, power seats, stereo equipment and even tape players, to say nothing of the electrical current required to run the engine and the headlights, windshield wipers, etc.), there is probably no single part of your car's equipment that is going to be placed under more stress and strain than that small black box that just sits there, day in and day out, not moving but constantly putting out the power that makes almost everything else on your car move. In order that it can continue to put out the impressive supply of electricity that your car and its equipment constantly demands, it is essential that there is a plentiful store of reserve current always in the battery. This used to be obtained from the car's generator until just a few years ago.

Today's new cars have almost all discarded the old-fashioned generator in favor of what is called an alternator. It is important that you should know the differences between these very important components. Very few motorists and quite a number of people who sell new cars are not aware of one very vital difference. It is to this that I will now address myself so that you can save yourself some inconvenience.

The old style generator would constantly charge the car's battery no matter how much or how little of the car's equipment was in use. You more mature folks will recall that several years back, whenever you had your headlights on (and perhaps the car's radio playing), the ampere meter on the dash would show a discharge, or if your car was not blessed with an ampere meter, the little red "idiot" light would come on, especially when the car was brought to a halt at the traffic lights or just standing at the curb with the engine idling. Today's cars do not do this unless something is wrong with the alternator, the battery, or the voltage regulator.

This is the most important benefit that these new alternators have brought to the motorist. Provided that the car's electrical system is in good working order, the alternator will immediately replace all of the electrical current drawn from the battery just as long as the engine is running. Even with the car standing still and the engine just slowly turning over, today's motorist can enjoy the services of his headlights, air conditioning, radio equipment and everything else on the car that uses electrical current, without taking more out of the battery than is being replaced by his alternator.

However, there is one thing lacking with this modern miracle. The alternator will not recharge the battery as the old style generator did. In the olden days, if you found your car would not start because your battery was *flat*, all you had to do was get someone to help you get the car started with a set of battery cables and then after you had driven the car for 10 or fifteen miles, a healthy generator would recharge the battery and you would probably have no further trouble. In today's cars, if your battery goes *flat*, you can start the car with the cables as before, but even if you drive it for 50 miles without switching off the engine, when you come to start the car again, you almost certainly find that the battery is still lifeless.

Many of today's new cars stand for months on the dealership's storage lots before they are sold and delivered to their new owner. Even the most minuscule short circuit in the electrical system of the car will cause a slow drain on the car's battery, and by the time the car is brought from the storage lot and delivered to the customer, almost all of the battery's reserve of electrical current has been exhausted. Often there is sufficient current left to start the car at the dealership so that the new owner can drive his new pride and joy for the rest of that first day, but if that slow drain from the short in the system continues overnight, the following morning will find a very disappointed and annoyed new car buyer trying to start his new car with a dead battery.

Here is my advice: Have the dealership where you buy your new car undertake to put the car's battery on slow charge for a couple of hours while the car is being serviced. They will be happy to do this if you ask them as the cost is negligible. However, it has been my experience that this service will not be given unless the customer demands it as a condition of buying the car. You'll find that this is a worthwhile tip and it might very well spare you the embarrassment of having to ask that envious neighbour to take the smirk off his face while he gives you some help with your brand new car on the very first morning you try to start it.

The rest of the battery warranty is alright, provided that you understand that it is fully guaranteed for just 12,000 miles or 1 year, whichever comes first. After that time or mileage period has elapsed, you will have to pay a portion of its replacement price, depending on the amount of unexpired warranty time. In any case, the battery warranty expires altogether 3 years from the date you bought the new car, after which if you need a new battery, you'll have to pay for the whole thing. Just remember that the battery's warranty is null and void if it's failure can be attributed to your negligence in not keeping the drinking water levels above the top of the plates, if you ever have cause to remove it and fail to reinstall it properly, use anything other than battery grade sulphuric acid solution of the specific gravity recommended by the manufacturer, or if in extreme temperatures you allow the battery to freeze up.

You have just finished reading what is probably the only comprehensive explanation of a typical new car warranty you will be likely to find. It has taken many pages to expand into clear layman's terms exactly what the manufacturers mean in their much more concisely worded document. You will find that, by and large, they will honor their end of the bargain *provided* (and that's the operative word) that you maintain your responsibility with regard to their service and maintenance demands.

11

ACCIDENTS, BODY REPAIRS, AND INSURANCE CLAIMS

No book on automobile repairs can be called complete without some comments on one other major cause of repair expense—body and paint damage. In our urban areas, where everything from minor scratches to major smashes are an everyday occurrence, there is probably almost as much money spent by motorists on having their exterior damage repaired and painted as there is on engine repairs and adjustments.

Anything which results in damage to the exterior of a car can be described as an accident. In most instances, where the cost of repair is less than $100, the motorist himself pays the tab. As most people carry either $50 or $100 deductable collision insurance, the insurance companies and their adjusters are involved whenever the damages amount to more than these deductable cushions. In as simple terms as we can muster, let us examine the whole process of being involved in a normal everyday kind of traffic accident. Nothing too serious. Let's assume that you are compelled to make an emergency stop and the car behind you runs into your tail, damaging your car's rear bumper and part of the coachwork including the trunk lid. Many motorists whose damaged cars are towed into the dealership with which I am associated, seem to have no idea of what to do when something like this happens to them. Many others think they know and as a result, leap out of their car as soon as any kind of collision occurs, and commence upbraiding and accusing the driver of the other car as if the whole thing had been a carefully planned vindictive attack. All kinds of lovely fun starts whenever an accident involves two such drivers and although the onlookers have a fine time watching the show, nothing is ever accomplished by this type of attitude.

I have been involved in just one accident that I can recall. It was on a high-speed freeway in the Los Angeles area and I had moved over into the slow lane so that I might get off the freeway at the next exit. The line of cars in the slow lane were just crawling along and coming to a brief halt every hundred yards or so as the exit ahead caused something of a bottleneck. I spotted a very ancient car just behind me; I remember wishing he wouldn't stay quite so close to my rear. The next time the line of cars came to a stop, the old car behind me did not. There I was, sitting quite uninjured, but with the trunk of my almost-new car caved in. Through my rear view mirror, I saw a fairly large man emerge from behind the wheel of the old turkey that had partly filled my car's luggage compartment with it's grille and radiator. He came up and leaned into my car until his ugly and smelly countenance was intolerably close and snarled, "Have you been driving for very long?"

He picked on the wrong man of course. I slid across the seat so that I could get out of my car on the side where there was no traffic. Under the seat of every car I have owned during the past seven or eight years, I have always kept a Polaroid Land camera just in case this kind of situation ever occurred. An old timer in the insurance business gave me this tip many years ago and I think it's worth passing on to you. It serves two purposes. It allows you to gather irrefutable evidence at

the scene of an accident, and it's a much better place to store
your camera than to leave it cluttering up your closet at home.
I took one picture of the line of traffic stopped in front of my
car, being careful to include the nose of my car, then I went
behind and to the side of his car and took a picture of the accident, making sure that his license plate was clearly visible
and that the line of traffic was in the background. By this
time, he had come to realize just what I was up to and as he
came striding angrily towards me, I took a beautiful picture
of him in all of his fury.

The line of cars behind us now stretched out of sight and
the cars in the next lane were, of course, all slowing down as
they passed to enjoy the fun. The comforting sound of a police
siren was getting closer every second and as my adversary
heard it, he seemed to come apart at the seams. He ran to his
old car, climbed in and started the engine. He was desperately
trying to disentangle his car from mine as the Highway
Patrol officer arrived on his motor cycle. Right on his heels
came another officer and they soon had him out of his car and
standing quietly at the side of the road. With the help of one
officer, we got both cars off the highway and on to the verge.
Then we stood in a small group while one of the officers made
out a report on the accident. We both told our version of the
story and surprisingly enough, when faced with the officer's
questions, our friend's story grudgingly admitted his liability.
When asked, I produced my current driver's license and insurance details. The other driver, when asked for his, con-
fessed that he had no insurance coverage and that his driver's
license had been suspended for drunk driving several months
previously.

In my one and only accident, I happened to be fortunate
and after many weeks, received a check in full settlement for
the damage to my car. However, just supposing the other guy
had had his driver's license and current insurance coverage,
he might not have so readily admitted his guilt and it might

have turned into one of those long drawn out affairs that almost always end in a stand-off with each participant paying to repair his own car.

At this point I must go back to that little tip I gave you regarding the camera. I sincerely hope that you are never involved in a collision while driving your automobile, but if you ever are, I'd like to think that you were one of my nice readers who took my advice and had your camera right there under the seat of your car, with a film at the ready, to record all the evidence you will ever need to support your side of the story. Ask yourself where your camera is right now. Supposing it was under the front seat of your car instead, would it be any less safe or convenient? If you have a very expensive camera and you like to keep it in your home, then consider investing in the lowest priced Polaroid Land camera. I understand you can get one nowadays for less than $20 and that's a small enough addition to your insurance premiums when you consider the corroboration it might one day give to your version of a traffic accident.

If you now carry comprehensive insurance coverage on your present car, ask your insurance agent to tell you how to act, what to say and what not to say and what your legal rights and limitations are and follow his instructions to the letter if ever you are involved in a traffic accident. Many insurance companies produce excellent small pamphlets giving the very best kind of advice to their customers on what to do if ever a collision should occur. Try and get hold of one of these and after you have studied it carefully, keep it in the glove box of your car so that you can refer to it right on the spot, should you ever need it.

If your car is ever immobilized after an accident on the highway, you are going to require the services of a tow truck and it's driver in order to have what is left of your car pulled to a garage for repairs. If this happens when you are driving on a side street or along one of our out of town highways, you will almost surely have to walk to the nearest telephone in order to summon some assistance. If the accident happens on one of the fast moving freeways which cut through all of the major cities nowadays, tow trucks will appear as if by magic from everywhere. Freeway accidents have become so common nowadays, that freelance tow truck operators find it quite profitable just to prowl along the freeways like a taxi, waiting for an accident to happen.

Some of these freeway tow truck operators act more like old time highwaymen if they find that a prospective client is in any way naive. Watch out for the guy who comes roaring up to the accident location, skids his truck to a halt in front of your car and with a friendly wave, asks if you need some help. Very often, if you say that you do, he will hurriedly back his truck up to your car and after hitching it up and lifting either the front or the rear of your car off the ground, he will then switch off his engine and get out of his cab with a contract in his hand ready to deal with you. The reason this type of character will connect up to your car and lift it first is that once this has been done and the police arrive on the scene, they will not chase him away and send for a tow truck from one of the garages on their list of recommended establishments.

Some of the independent prowlers have been the subject of complaints from outraged individuals who have later informed the authorities that they were coerced into signing an agreement which they were both unable and unwilling to read thoroughly while standing at the side of a rainy, darkened or windy freeway. Only later did they discover that that nice, friendly, and helpful tow truck man was really a gangster disguised as a truck driver. Not only were they compelled to pay about double the normal fee to the driver in cash and *in advance*, they had also signed an agreement to have the car stored at this guy's yard until the repairs could be started at a rate something like 3 times the generally accepted scale for car storage. There is very little the police can do about this. After all, there is nothing wrong with a man selling his services for as much as he can get.

In most states, the police authorities try to get to the scene of an accident before the tow truck sharks arrive. Then they try to be helpful to the unfortunate motorist by using their two way radio to summon a truck from one of the more ethically run garages on their list. When the accident chasers arrive, the officer can then quite legitimately wave them off by telling them that a truck has already been sent for.

Watch out for this, especially those of you who have not been involved in an accident in a long time. It's such a miserable experience, I know, standing there at the side of the road with the whole world sweeping past in the cosy security of their cars. They don't even bother to glance at you as you stand praying that some kindly soul will stop and offer to help. When that tow truck appears and pulls over beside you, you feel that your prayers have been answered, especially when the driver starts out by being so friendly. So here's my advice. If the traffic is reasonably busy, you'll not have to wait very long for a patrolling officer to arrive, so be patient until he comes along. If a tow truck stops and asks if you need help, thank him but tell him that you've already sent for a truck and it is on the way. Whatever you do, never allow him to hitch his truck to your car or all is lost. A minute will seem like an hour while you are standing beside your car and feeling upset, but just remember that if the local police department patrol that road at all, one of their friendly and helpful officers will arrive if you have patience.

What about those body and paint repairs? Boy, they're expensive nowadays. The price of this kind of work seems to have just about doubled within the past few years. There are 3 types of body shops in most towns. The most obvious one is the new car dealership's operation, and as a general rule, this is where you will get the best quality work done. By no means will it be the cheapest, but if the insurance company is going to pick up most of the tab, the new car dealership would be my first choice. Their operators are usually the most skilled also, as they are kept busy all of the time because of the connections most new car dealerships with the local insurance adjusters. It's a kind of you-scratch-my-back-and-I'll-scratch-yours arrangement. A dealership selling new cars is a very nice connection for an aggressive insurance man to have, and by using a little hanky-panky, the adjuster can see to it that a new car dealership's body shop can benefit by a continuous stream of accident repair jobs. Thus, as body and paint workers are paid on a flat rate scale, the best of them will naturally work where the most work and the highest charges are available.

In most towns, you will also find the fairly good quality establishment which tries to compete with the new car dealerships, by charging a little less. The best of these are quite good, but if your car is fairly extensively damaged, it will not be possible to drive it from place to place, in an attempt to find the best deal. The insurance adjuster will probably tell you to obtain 2 or 3 bids on the work you need and bring them in to him. He might even tell you the name of one place he would like you to go for a bid, and you'll find that the place he mentions is almost always one of the local new car dealerships. More about why he does this after we tell you about the third and last type of body and paint repair shop that will be available to you.

This is the cut-rate operation. They will probably advertise extensively in your local newspapers and on radio. Almost without exception, the work here is hurried and of poor quality. Not only will your car be painted, but your tires, bumpers, and windows might also be given a generous coating. This kind of place is alright if you are just trying to smarten up an old car, or if you cannot afford anything better, but from the experiences I have had in the past when attempting to save a dollar or two, I cannot recommend that you patronize such a place.

Getting back to the new car dealership and the insurance adjuster. Don't be surprised if the adjuster sanctions your needed repairs to be done at the highest bidder, if that is where he is getting his extra business from. This shouldn't concern you as all you want is for the work to be properly done. It's going to cost you only your $50 or $100 deductable anyway, so why should you care? I bring it up only to show you that here is at least 1 reason why the cost of our automobile insurance is getting higher every year. There is even collusion between competing dealerships in this same area. The insurance adjuster sends you out to get 3 bids on your accident repairs and at the very first new car dealership you call, the estimator asks where else you've been. You tell him that his is the first estimate you've asked for and he might tell you that he can save you a lot of driving and waiting around if you're interested. Of course you are only interested in getting the work started on your car as soon as possible so you are ready to be a party to a little finagling. This is what will happen if you ever ask for an insurance estimate at a place like this. After completing and pricing the list of new parts required and entering the labor charges on the estimate sheet with his own dealership's printed heading, he will ask you to follow him into his office, where he will sit down and produce 2 more blank estimate sheets, each with a competing dealership's name and address printed at the top. He will complete each of these by copying the needed parts and labor from his original sheet. When he gets around to entering the charges, he will make these a little more on his competitors sheets and end up by handing you 3 perfectly legitimate estimates from 3 different dealerships which could never be even doubted by an insurance adjuster.

As a result of this little piece of larceny, his shop will get the job and you will be spared the chore of driving to 2 more places and waiting around while the estimates are prepared. Not every new car dealership will be a party to this, but more and more of them are "joining up" all the time. More often than not the new car dealers themselves are unaware that this is going on in their place of business, and it's next to impossible for them to find out about it. You will recall from an earlier chapter, that service managers, and automobile repairmen are usually compensated on a share of the profits basis these days, so the higher they can fix their prices for any particular job, the larger the paycheck they are going to pull in.

Estimators and body shop managers usually get to know each other in any given area and it's quite common for them to have a cup of coffee together and set up profitable joint ventures which sometimes result in a few pads of their dealership's estimate sheets being exchanged. Just remember that this outrage could not be perpetrated without the help and co-operation of Mr. and Mrs. John Q. Public. It would be quite revealing to discover just how much even this one pricing device adds to our insurance premiums each year.

YOUR OWN
FLAT RATE BOOK

YOUR OWN FLAT RATE BOOK

Passenger cars.

Suggested maintenance.

	Hours
LUBRICATION	
Chassis—lubricate complete. Includes: Lubricate all connections with high-pressure fittings, clutch linkage, distributor, and accelerator; check steering gear lubricants, transmission, and rear axle, and add where required; check tire pressures and battery water levels. All models	0.4
Combinations:	
Automatic transmissions. Drain and refill	0.3
Standard transmissions. Drain and refill	0.1
Rear axle. Drain and refill	0.2
Engine oil. Change	0.2
Oil filter. Replace	0.1
Body and hood lubrication. Includes: Lubricate door locks, hinges, striker plates; check links and wedge plates, hood locks and hood hinges	0.3
Oil filter. Replace	0.2
Automatic transmission. Drain and refill	0.4
Standard transmission. Drain and refill	0.2
Rear axle. Drain and refill	0.3
Speedometer cable. Lubricate	0.2
Front wheel bearings. Repack	0.6
FRONT SUSPENSION	
Front wheel toe-in. Adjust	0.4
Front end alignment. Check	0.5
Front end alignment. Check and correct	1.2
Front wheel bearing. Adjust	0.3
Headlamps. Aim	0.3

Hours

BRAKES

Brake main cylinder. Check and add fluid	0.2
Brake system. Pressure bleed	0.4
Brake system. Flush	0.9
Brake shoes. Front only. Grind	1.0
Brake shoes. Rear. Grind	0.4
Brake drum (each). Reface	0.3

ADJUSTMENTS

Engine tune-up. Includes: Check engine compression; clean or replace and adjust distributor points; clean and adjust spark plugs; test battery; clean terminals; check distributor rotor and cap; check manual and vacuum ignition advance and set timing; check manifold heat control; test coil and condenser and air cleaner; normalize engine; adjust carburetor idle; tighten hose connections and adjust fan belts. Does not include testing voltage regulator or overhauling carburetor. All six-cylinder models 1.7

All eight-cylinders	2.5
Carburetor. Adjust idling speed and mixture	0.2
Valves. Adjust, all six-cylinders	0.5
Valves. Adjust, all V8s	0.7
If equipped with air conditioning, add	0.3
Ignition timing and dwell angle. Adjust	0.3

Spark plugs (all). Clean and adjust or replace. All six-cylinder engines 0.3

All V8 engines	0.6
All V8 engines with air conditioning	1.3
Voltage regulator. Test and adjust	0.5
Battery. Starting and charging circuits. Diagnosis	0.4
Battery terminals. Clean	0.2

Air emission control check. Includes: Adjust carburetor idle speed, fuel mixture, and engine timing; check operation of positive crankcase ventilation valve and replace if needed 0.4

Air cleaner element. Clean and replace	0.2
Cooling system. Flush	0.5
Cooling system. Clean and reverse flush	1.5
Drive belts. Each belt	0.2

TRANSMISSIONS

Clutch linkage. Adjust. Includes: Raise and lower vehicle; loosen and tighten adjusting nut; measure pedal free travel 0.2

Shift linkage. Adjust	0.2
Throttle valve linkage. Adjust	0.2

FUEL
Gasoline tank. Clean internally 1.5
Gasoline pipes (all). Clean 0.5

STEERING
Steering gear assembly. Adjust in vehicle 0.6
If equipped with tilt-type steering column, add 0.3
Steering gear. Set on high point 0.3
Power steering. Diagnosis 0.4

WHEELS AND TIRES
Rotate all 0.6
Wheel balance. One wheel 0.3
Four wheels 0.8
If necessary to remove wheel assembly, add for each wheel .. 0.1

AIR CONDITIONING
Performance test 0.4
Thermostatic switch. Adjust 0.3
Leak check 0.3
Air conditioning system. Charge (includes performance test
    and leak check) 1.4

COWL AND DASH ASSEMBLY
Windshield glass. Replace. Includes: R & R (remove and re-
    place) wiper arms; R & R all moldings; reseal and water
    test. All cars except convertibles 1.6
All convertibles 2.2
If necessary to replace caulking, add 0.4
Windshield glass. Reseal. Includes: R & R moldings and wa-
    ter test. 0.5
Convertibles 0.9
When necessary to remove lower reveal molding, add 0.3

HARDWARE
Molding. Windshield garnish. Replace complete 0.3
Convertibles 0.4
Molding. Windshield garnish. Right side. Replace 0.2
Convertibles 0.3
Molding. Windshield garnish. Upper. Replace 0.2
Convertibles 0.3
Molding. Windshield reveal. Replace complete 0.3
Convertibles 0.7

Hours

Molding. Windshield reveal. Upper. Replace 0.2
Convertibles 0.6
Molding. Windshield reveal. Side. Replace 0.2
Convertibles 0.6
Molding. Windshield reveal. Lower. Replace 0.2
Convertibles 0.6
Molding. Windshield header. Replace complete 0.5
Molding. Windshield pillar finishing. Replace 0.6
Molding. Windshield header. Replace 1.3
Mirror. Rear view (inside) 0.2
Lock assembly. Instrument panel compartment. Replace 0.2
Box assembly. Instrument panel compartment. Replace 0.3
Door assembly. Instrument panel compartment. Replace. Includes: Transfer lock cylinder assembly. 0.3

TRIM
Cover assembly. Instrument panel. Replace 0.9
If equipped with air conditioning, add 0.3

HEATER
Heater assembly. Remove and reinstall. Includes: Drain and refill radiator; remove and replace heater hoses, glove box and door, bowden cables and electrical connections, firewall to heater mounting nuts 1.0
If with air conditioning, as above, plus remove and replace right front fender skirt, battery and tray, radio, heater control assembly, and center console when necessary 2.4
Heater control assembly. Replace. Includes: D & C (disconnect and connect) battery cable; remove and replace instrument panel bezel, control panel screws, and bowden cables; D & C all electrical connections 0.6
Heater blower resistor unit. Replace 0.3
Heater blower switch. Replace 0.5
Heater blower motor. Replace 1.1
Heater hoses. Replace. Includes: Drain and refill radiator 0.4
If air conditioning 0.6

AIR CONDITIONING
Compressor assembly. Replace. Includes: Purge; remove and replace compressor connector block and compressor; transfer mounting brackets, clutch hub and drive plate assembly, coil housing, pulley and bearing assembly; evacuate, recharge; performance and leak test system 2.5

	Hours
Compressor hub and drive plate. Replace. Six-cylinder models	0.6
V8 models	0.5
Compressor pulley and bearing. Replace	0.7
Compressor coil housing assembly	0.7
Compressor shaft seal assembly	2.4
If necessary to add oil to compressor, add	0.7
Compressor relief valve. Replace	1.5
Compressor rear reed assembly. Includes: Purge; D & C charging fitting block and muffler assembly from compressor; R & R compressor from engine; R & R rear head and reed plate assembly, clean and inspect parts; evacuate, recharge; performance and leak test system	2.4
Compressor front reed assembly. Replace	3.4
Compressor assembly. Overhaul	5.1
Condenser. Replace	2.4
Sight glass. Replace	1.4
Receiver-dehydrator. Replace	1.6
Evaporator. Replace	2.9
Evaporator case. Replace	3.2
Expansion valve. Replace	2.7
Thermostatic switch. Replace	0.3
Air conditioning blower motor. Replace	2.7
Air conditioning blower motor switch. Replace	0.7
Air conditioning resistor. Replace	0.4
Air conditioning relay. Replace	0.2
Air conditioning clutch switch. Replace	0.7
Air condition temperature switch. Replace	0.2
Air conditioning control assembly. Replace	1.0
Thermal vacuum valve. Replace	0.3
Vacuum tank. Replace	0.6
Defroster cable. Replace	0.9
Diverter door cable. Replace	1.7
Air conditioning line valve to compressor. Replace	1.8
Hoses, fittings, and muffler assembly. Replace	1.7
Air conditioning line, condenser to dehydrator. Replace	1.6

FRONT SUSPENSION (Time allowances for front end alignment not included.)

Steering knuckles. Replace	0.8
Spherical joint assemblies. Replace. Upper. One side	0.6
Upper. Both sides	1.1
Lower. One side	0.8
Lower. Both sides	1.5

Upper and lower. One side	1.1
Upper and lower. Both sides	2.3
Upper control arms. Replace. One side	0.9
Both sides	1.8
Lower control arms. Replace. One side	0.9
Both sides	1.7
Upper control arm bushings. Replace. One side	0.9
Both sides	1.7
Lower control arm bushings. Replace. One side	1.4
Both sides	2.6
Upper control arm rubber bumpers. Replace. One side	0.2
Both sides	0.3
Lower control arm rubber bumpers. Replace. One side	0.2
Both sides	0.3
Strut rod and/or bushings. Replace. One side	0.4
Both sides	0.6
Front wheel hub. Replace. One side	0.5
Both sides	0.8
If with disc brakes, for each wheel add	0.2

FRONT WHEEL BEARINGS

Front wheel outer bearing assembly. Replace. One side	0.5
Both sides	0.7
With disc brakes. One side	0.8
With disc brakes. Both sides	1.3
Front wheel inner bearing assembly. Replace. One side	0.5
Both sides	0.8
With disc brakes. One side	0.7
With disc brakes. Both sides	1.3
Front wheel bearing oil seal. Replace. One side.	0.4
Both sides	0.7
With disc brakes. One side	0.6
With disc brakes. Both sides	1.2
Front wheel bearing assemblies (inner and outer). Replace.	
One side	0.5
Both sides	0.8
With disc brakes. One side	0.7
With disc brakes. Both sides	1.3

FRONT SPRINGS

Front springs. Replace. One side	1.2
Both sides	2.3

SHOCK ABSORBERS	*Hours*
Front shock absorbers. Replace. One side	0.3
Both sides	0.5

FRONT STABILIZER

Front stabilizer shaft. Replace	0.7
Front stabilizer shaft bushings. Replace	0.4
Front stabilizer link bolts and/or grommets. Replace	0.4

REAR SUSPENSION

Differential case assembly. Remove and reinstall	2.0
Pinion shaft oil seal (front). Replace	0.8
Pinion shaft oil seal (rear). Replace	4.5

REAR AXLE SHAFTS AND BEARINGS

Axle shaft. Replace. One side	0.7
Both sides	1.1
Axle shaft bearings and/or oil seals. Replace. One side	0.7
Both sides	1.0
Axle shaft flange studs. Replace. One side	0.9
Both sides	1.3

REAR AXLE HOUSING

Rear axle housing. Replace	4.2
Rear axle housing cover gasket. Replace	0.4

PROPELLER SHAFT

Propeller shaft. Remove and reinstall	0.4

REAR SPRINGS

Rear springs. Replace. One side	0.8
Both sides	1.0
Rear upper control arm. Replace. One side	0.6
Both sides	1.1
Rear lower control arm. Replace. One side	1.1
Both sides	1.7
Rear suspension tie rod assembly. Replace	0.3
Rear suspension tie rod stud. Replace	0.3
Rebound bumper. Replace	0.3

SHOCK ABSORBERS

Rear shock absorbers. Replace. One side	0.3
Both sides	0.5

BRAKES

	Hours
Brake shoes (all). Replace. With disc brakes	1.8
With standard brakes	2.2
Brake self-adjuster (each). Overhaul or replace	0.4
Return springs (one wheel). Replace	0.4

FRONT BRAKES AND DRUMS

Brake backing plate. Front. Replace one. Standard brakes	1.1
Brake shoes, except with disc brakes. Replace	1.0
Brake shoes with disc brakes. Replace both front wheels	0.8
Brake wheel cylinder. Front. Replace or overhaul	1.0
Brake wheel cylinder. Front. Replace both	1.6
Brake caliper assembly. Front. Remove and replace. One side	0.6
Both sides	0.9
Brake drums. Front. Remove and replace. Each	0.5
Brake disc. Front. Remove and replace both	1.1

REAR BRAKES AND DRUMS

Brake backing plate. Rear. Replace one	1.4
Brake shoes (both rear wheels). Replace	1.1
Brake wheel cylinder. Rear. Replace or overhaul. One	1.0
Both	1.6
Brake drums. Rear. Remove and replace. Each	0.4
Brake pedal push rod to main cylinder clearance. Adjust	0.3
Brake pedal, bushings or return spring. Replace	0.5
Parking brake cable. Rear. Replace	0.7
Parking brake cable. Intermediate. Replace	0.3
Parking brake cable. Front. Replace	0.9
Parking brake control and ratchet assembly. Replace	0.3
Parking brake cable return spring. Replace	0.2
Parking brake equalizer. Replace	0.3
Brake master cylinder. Replace	0.3
Brake pressure differential warning switch. Replace	0.5
Brake hoses. Front or rear (one only). Replace	0.4
Brake pipe. Main cylinder to switch. Replace	0.5
Brake pipe distribution and switch assembly. Replace	0.7
Brake pipe switch to front wheel flex hose. Replace left side ..	0.7
Replace right side	0.9
Brake pipe front to rear intermediate. Replace	1.0
Brake pipe intermediate to rear wheels. Replace	0.7
Power brake power cylinder. Replace	0.5
Power brake vacuum hose or check valve. Replace	0.2

ENGINE ASSEMBLY

Engine assembly. Replace. Six Cylinders	4.6
Engine assembly. Replace. Eight cylinders	6.0

Hours

Cylinder block assembly (short engine). Replace. Six cylinders	8.4
Eight cylinders	10.5
With power steering, add	0.4
With air conditioning, add	0.5
Cylinder block (fitted). Replace. Six cylinders	10.9
Eight cylinders	14.5
With power steering, add	0.3
With air conditioning, add	0.5
Cylinder head. Replace. Six cylinders	4.1
Eight cylinders. Replace one bank	5.6
Eight cylinders. Replace both banks	8.5
With power steering, add	0.3
With air conditioning, if compressor must be disconnected, add	0.6
Cylinder head gasket. Replace. Six cylinders	2.5
Eight cylinders. One bank	4.2
Eight cylinders. Both banks	6.9
With power steering, add	0.3
With air conditioning, if compressor must be disconnected, add	0.6
Crankshaft. Replace. Six cylinders	6.4
Eight cylinders	8.8
With power steering, add	0.3
With air conditioning, if compressor must be disconnected, add	0.6
Rear main bearing oil seal. Replace. Six cylinders	2.6
Eight cylinders	2.5
Main bearings. Replace one. Six cylinders	2.9
Eight cylinders	2.6
Connecting rod. Replace one. Six cylinders	6.0
Eight cylinders	7.6
With power steering, add	0.3
With air conditioning, if compressor must be disconnected, add	0.6
Connecting rods. Replace all. Six cylinders	8.3
Eight cylinders	10.5
With power steering, add	0.3
With air conditioning, if compressor must be disconnected, add	0.6
Connecting rod bearing. Replace one. Six cylinders	2.8
Eight cylinders	3.4
Connecting rod bearings. Replace all. Six cylinders	4.2
Eight cylinders	3.9
Piston or piston and cylinder assembly (one). Replace. Six cylinders	6.3
Eight cylinders	6.7

Hours

With power steering, add	0.3
With air conditioning, if compressor must be disconnected, add	0.6
Piston or piston and cylinder assemblies (all). Replace. Six cylinders	7.9
Eight cylinders	10.8
With power steering, add	0.3
With air conditioning, if compressor must be disconnected, add	0.6
Piston rings (one piston). Replace. Six-cylinder engines	6.1
Eight-cylinder engines	6.6
Piston rings (all). Replace. Six-cylinder engines	8.4
Eight-cylinder engines	10.7
With power steering, add	0.3
With air conditioning, if compressor must be dismounted, add	0.6
Valves. Grind. Six-cylinder engines	4.5
Eight-cylinder engines. One bank	5.6
Eight-cylinder engines. Both banks	9.4
With power steering, add	0.3
With air conditioning, if compressor must be removed, add ..	0.6
Valve rocker arms. Replace. Six-cylinder engines. One, two, or three	0.5
Six-cylinder engines. Four, five, or six	0.7
Eight-cylinder engines. Any or all of one bank	0.6
Eight-cylinder engines. Any or all of both banks	1.3
Eight-cylinder engines equipped with air conditioning, for left bank only add	0.4
Valve lifter. Replace one. Six-cylinder engines	0.7
Eight-cylinder engines. Replace one	1.6
Valve lifters. Replace all. Six-cylinder engines	1.3
Eight-cylinder engines	3.3
Eight-cylinder engines with air conditioning, add	0.4
Valve seal. Replace one. Six-cylinder engines	0.7
Eight-cylinder engines	0.7
Eight-cylinder engines equipped with air conditioning, for left bank only add	0.4
Valve rocker arm cover gasket. Replace. Six-cylinder engines	0.4
Eight-cylinder engines. One bank	0.3
Eight-cylinder engines. Both banks	0.5
Eight-cylinder engines equipped with air conditioning, for left bank only add	0.4
Oil pan gasket. Replace. Six-cylinder engines	2.2
Eight-cylinder engines	1.9

	Hours
Oil pump. Replace. Six-cylinder engines	2.6
Eight-cylinder engines	1.8
Oil filter. Replace	0.2
Crankcase ventilation valve adaptor. Replace	0.2
Crankcase ventilation tee and/or nipple. Replace	0.2
Crankcase ventilation valve assembly. Replace	0.2
Crankcase ventlation hose. Replace	0.2
Timing cover gasket. Replace. Six cylinders	2.8
Eight cylinders	2.6
With power steering, add	0.2
With air conditioning, add	0.2
Timing cover oil seal. Replace. Six-cylinder engines	0.8
Eight-cylinder engines	0.6
Torsional damper. Replace. Six cylinders	0.8
Eight cylinders	0.5
With power steering, add	0.1
Camshaft. Replace. Six-cylinder engines	7.6
Eight-cylinder engines	6.4
(Add time allowance for engines with power steering, air conditioning, or automatic transmission.)	
Camshaft gear. Replace. Six-cylinder engines	7.4
Eight-cylinder engines	4.2
(Add time allowance for power steering, air conditioning, or automatic transmission.)	
Timing chain. Replace	4.1
Drive belts. Replace one belt	0.2
Fan. Replace	0.3
Fan pulley. Replace. One belt	0.4
Fan pulley. Replace. Two belts	0.5
Fan pulley. Replace. Three belts	0.6
Air cleaner. Replace	0.2
Fuel pump. Replace. Six-cylinder engines	0.3
Eight-cylinder engines	0.4
Fuel pump push rod. Replace	0.7
Carburetor bowl cover. Remove and reinstall. One carburetor	0.6
Two carburetors	0.7
Four carburetors	1.3
Carburetor floats. Adjust	0.5
Carburetor floats. Replace one	0.6
Replace both	1.0
Carburetor needle and seats. Replace each	0.4
Carburetor. Replace	0.7
Carburetor. Overhaul. One carburetor	1.2

	Hours
Two carburetors	1.9
Four carburetors	3.1
Automatic choke thermostat and/or lower rod. Replace	0.4
Engine mounts. Front. Replace. Six-cylinder engines. One side	0.3
Six-cylinder engines. Both sides	0.4
Eight-cylinder engines. One side	0.6
Eight-cylinder engines. Both sides	1.1
With power steering, add	0.3
Engine mounts. Rear. Replace	0.5
Water pump gaskets. Replace. Six cylinders	0.8
Eight cylinders	1.0
Radiator hoses. Replace. Upper	0.3
Radiator hoses. Replace. Lower	0.4
Radiator hoses. Replace. Both	0.5
Thermostat. Replace	0.4
Thermostat housing. Replace	0.4
Thermostat housing gasket. Replace	0.4
Manifold gaskets. Replace. Six-cylinder engines	0.6
Eight-cylinder engines	1.6
Intake manifold. Replace. Six cylinders	1.0
Intake manifold. Replace. Eight cylinders	2.3
With power steering, add	0.3
With air conditioning, add	0.3
Exhaust manifold. Replace. Six cylinders	1.0
Eight cylinders	1.0
With power steering, add	0.3
With air conditioning, add	0.4

ELECTRICAL

Starter motor. Remove and reinstall or replace. Six-cylinder engines	0.5
Eight-cylinder engines	0.7
Voltage regulator. Test and adjust	0.5
Voltage regulator. Test and replace	0.4
Ignition coil. Replace	0.3
Distributor cap. Replace	0.2
Distributor rotor. Replace	0.2
Distributor points. Replace. Six cylinders	0.4
Eight cylinders	0.5
Distributor condenser. Replace	0.2
Vacuum advance assembly. Replace. Six cylinders	0.3
Eight cylinders	0.5
Distributor. Remove and reinstall	0.6

	Hours
Distributor-to-coil primary wire. Replace	0.2
Spark plug wires (all). Replace	0.5
Spark plugs (all). Clean and adjust or replace. Six-cylinder engines	0.3
Eight-cylinder engines	0.6

FUEL SYSTEMS

Gasoline tank. Replace	1.1
Gasoline tank straps. Replace	0.5
Gasoline vent pipe hose. Replace	0.2
Gasoline tank vent pipe. Replace	0.4
Gasoline tank filler neck and vent pipe. Replace	0.4
Gasoline pipe hoses. Replace	0.3
Gasoline gauge (tank unit). Replace	0.9

EXHAUST SYSTEMS

Exhaust pipe and/or exhaust cross pipe. Replace. Single exhaust	0.5
Dual exhausts	0.8
Muffler. Replace. Single exhaust	0.6
Dual exhausts	0.9
Resonator and pipe assembly. Replace	0.6
Tail pipe. Replace. Each	0.5
Muffler rubber insulator and/or bracket. Replace. One side ..	0.4
Both sides	0.6

TRANSMISSIONS

Clutch pedal and/or bushings. Replace	0.5
Clutch pedal push rod and seal. Replace	0.4
Clutch push rod tension spring. Replace	0.2
Clutch cross shaft assembly. Replace	0.4
Clutch fork push rod assembly. Replace	0.4
Clutch return spring. Replace	0.2
Clutch pressure plate	1.9
Transmission assembly (3-speed). Remove and replace	1.5
Transmission side cover (3-speed). Replace	0.7
Transmission side cover gasket (3-speed). Replace	0.6
Transmission rear oil seal (3-speed). Replace	0.5
Transmission assembly (4-speed). Remove and replace	1.8
Transmission side cover (4-speed). Replace	0.7
Transmission side cover gasket (4-speed). Replace	0.6
Transmission rear oil seal (4-speed). Replace	0.5

Hours

Column shift selector lever and spring. Replace	1.1
Floor shift control lever. Replace	0.9
Floor shift control lever opening seals. Replace	0.4
Floor shift control lever assembly. Replace	0.8
Transmission shift rods (3-speed). Replace	0.4
Transmission shift rods (4-speed). Replace	0.6
Floor shift back drive rod or cable. Replace	0.3
Speedometer driven gear seal. Replace	0.2

AUTOMATIC TRANSMISSIONS

Column shift selector lever and spring. Replace	0.7
Throttle valve control rod. Replace	0.4
Shift control assembly. Replace	0.4
Floor shift control lever assembly. Replace	0.6
Automatic transmission assembly. Remove and replace	2.3
Transmission oil pan gasket. Replace	0.6
Transmission oil pan. Replace	0.7
Case extension housing gasket. Replace	0.7
Housing rear oil seal. Replace	0.6
Governor cover or gasket. Replace	0.5
Oil cooler pipes. Replace. One pipe	0.6
Both pipes	0.9
Vacuum modulator and seal. Replace	0.4
Valve body assembly. Replace	1.0
Valve body assembly. Overhaul	1.6
Throttle valve pressure. Adjust	0.7

STEERING

Steering gear assembly. Replace	0.6
Steering gear shaft seal. Replace	0.7
Steering flexible coupling. Replace	0.5
Steering column assembly. Remove and replace	1.3
Tilt steering column. Replace actuator	1.0
Steering shaft (tilt column). Replace upper	1.1
Mast jacket upper bearing. Replace	1.2
Steering wheel. Replace	0.3
Pitman arm. Replace	0.4
Steering idler arm. Replace	0.4
Steering knuckle arms. Replace. One side	0.8
Both sides	1.3
With disc brakes. One side	1.7
With disc brakes. Both sides	2.5
Tie rods. Replace. One	0.7

	Hours
Both	1.0
Power steering pump assembly. Replace	0.4
Power steering pump front mounting bracket. Replace. Six cylinders	0.6
Eight cylinders	0.5
Power steering pump rear bracket. Replace	0.3
Power steering pump pulley. Replace	0.3
Power steering hydraulic hoses. Replace. One	0.4
Both	0.6
Power steering pump flow control valve. Replace. Six cylinders	0.5
Eight cylinders	0.9
Power steering gear assembly. Remove and replace	0.9

ELECTRICAL

Battery. Remove and reinstall	0.2
Battery cables. Replace positive	0.4
Battery cables. Replace ground	0.2
Battery tray and/or support. Replace	0.4
Headlamp. Sealed beam unit. Replace	0.4
Lighting switch. Replace	0.3
Headlamp dimmer switch. Replace	0.3
Directional signal flasher unit. Replace	0.2
Parking lamp assembly. Replace. One side	0.3
Both sides	0.5
Automatic transmission neutral switch. Replace	0.3
Back-up lamp switch. Replace	0.4
Tail lamp assembly. Tail and stop. Replace. Each	0.3
License plate lamp assembly. Replace	0.2
Horn. Replace	0.3
Horn relay. Replace	0.2
Speedometer cable. Replace	0.5
With air conditioning. Replace	0.8
Cigar lighter assembly. Replace	0.4
Windshield wiper switch assembly. Replace	0.7
Windshield wiper motor assembly. Replace	0.4
With air conditioning, add	0.2
Windshield washer pump assembly. Replace	0.3

BUMPERS

Front bumper assembly. Remove and reinstall. If on extended brackets	0.5
If integral with body	1.1
Rear bumper assembly. Remove and reinstall. If on extended brackets	0.5

	Hours
If integral with body	0.8
Rear bumper valance. Replace	0.3
Rear bumper guard. Replace. One	0.2
Both	0.3
Radio and front speaker. Remove and replace	0.4
With air conditioning	0.7
Radio antenna rod. Replace	0.2
Radio antenna lead-in cable. Replace. Front	0.3
Rear	0.8
Wheel covers. Replace one or all	0.2
Door edge guards. Replace one set	0.3
Outside rear view mirror. Replace	0.2
Parking lamp (brakes) signal switch. Replace	0.3

Before having any repairs undertaken at your local new car dealership or garage, call them on the telephone and ask how much per hour they charge for labor. Then you can come very close to figuring your repair bill by using the tables set out below. Simply use the column under the hourly rate in effect at your garage. Thus, if the rate is $9.50 per hour and your needed repair is flat rated at 3.4 hours, you are going to be charged $32.30 for the mechanic's time, plus the full retail list price for any parts that are replaced.

Hours @	$6.50	7.00	7.50	8.00	8.50	9.00	9.50	10.00	10.50
0.1	.65	.70	.75	.80	.85	.90	.95	1.00	1.05
0.2	1.30	1.40	1.50	1.60	1.70	1.80	1.90	2.00	2.10
0.3	1.95	2.10	2.25	2.40	2.55	2.70	2.85	3.00	3.15
0.4	2.60	2.80	3.00	3.20	3.40	3.60	3.80	4.00	4.20
0.5	3.25	3.50	3.75	4.00	4.25	4.50	4.75	5.00	5.25
0.6	3.90	4.20	4.50	4.80	5.10	5.40	5.70	6.00	6.30
0.7	4.55	4.90	5.25	5.60	5.95	6.30	6.65	7.00	7.35
0.8	5.20	5.60	6.00	6.40	6.80	7.20	7.60	8.00	8.40
0.9	5.85	6.30	6.75	7.20	7.65	8.10	8.55	9.00	9.45
1.0	6.50	7.00	7.50	8.00	8.50	9.00	9.50	10.00	10.50
1.1	7.15	7.70	8.25	8.80	9.35	9.90	10.45	11.00	11.55
1.2	7.80	8.40	9.00	9.60	10.20	10.80	11.40	12.00	13.60
1.3	8.45	9.10	9.75	10.40	11.05	11.70	12.35	13.00	13.65
1.4	9.10	9.80	10.50	11.20	11.90	12.60	13.30	14.00	14.70
1.5	9.75	10.50	11.25	12.00	12.75	13.50	14.25	15.00	15.75
1.6	10.40	11.20	12.00	12.80	13.60	14.40	15.20	16.00	16.80
1.7	11.05	11.90	12.75	13.60	14.45	15.30	16.15	17.00	17.85
1.8	11.70	12.60	13.50	14.40	15.30	16.20	17.10	18.00	18.90
1.9	12.35	13.30	14.25	15.20	16.15	17.10	18.05	19.00	19.95
2.0	13.00	14.00	15.00	16.00	17.00	18.00	19.00	20.00	21.00

Hours @	$6.50	7.00	7.50	8.00	8.50	9.00	9.50	10.00	10.50
2.1	13.65	14.70	15.75	16.80	17.85	18.90	19.95	21.00	22.05
2.2	14.30	15.40	16.50	17.60	18.70	19.80	20.90	22.00	23.10
2.3	14.95	16.10	17.25	18.40	19.55	20.70	21.85	23.00	24.15
2.4	15.60	16.80	18.00	19.20	20.40	21.60	22.80	24.00	25.20
2.5	16.25	17.50	18.75	20.00	21.25	22.50	23.75	25.00	26.25
2.6	16.90	18.20	19.50	20.80	22.10	23.40	24.70	26.00	27.30
2.7	17.55	18.90	20.25	21.60	22.95	24.30	25.65	27.00	28.35
2.8	18.20	19.60	21.00	22.40	23.80	25.20	26.60	28.00	29.40
2.9	18.85	20.30	21.75	23.20	24.65	26.10	27.55	29.00	30.45
3.0	19.50	21.00	22.50	24.00	25.50	27.00	28.50	30.00	31.50
3.1	20.15	21.70	23.25	24.80	26.35	27.90	29.45	31.00	32.55
3.2	20.80	22.40	24.00	25.60	27.20	28.80	30.40	32.00	33.60
3.3	21.45	23.10	24.75	26.40	28.05	29.70	31.35	33.00	34.65
3.4	22.10	23.80	25.50	27.20	28.90	30.60	32.30	34.00	35.70
3.5	22.75	24.50	26.25	28.00	29.75	31.50	33.25	35.00	36.75
3.6	23.40	25.20	27.00	28.80	30.60	32.40	34.20	36.00	37.80
3.7	24.05	25.90	27.75	29.60	31.45	33.30	35.15	37.00	38.85
3.8	24.70	26.60	28.50	30.40	32.30	34.20	36.10	38.00	39.90
3.9	25.35	27.30	29.25	31.20	33.15	35.10	37.05	39.00	40.95
4.0	26.00	28.00	30.00	32.00	34.00	36.00	38.00	40.00	42.00
4.1	26.65	28.70	30.75	32.80	34.85	36.90	38.95	41.00	43.05
4.2	27.30	29.40	31.50	33.60	35.70	37.80	39.90	42.00	44.10
4.3	27.95	30.10	32.25	34.40	36.55	38.70	40.85	43.00	45.15
4.4	28.60	30.80	33.00	35.20	37.40	39.60	41.80	44.00	46.20
4.5	29.25	31.50	33.75	36.00	38.25	40.50	42.75	45.00	47.25
4.6	29.90	32.20	34.50	36.80	39.10	41.40	43.70	46.00	48.30
4.7	30.55	32.90	35.25	37.60	39.95	42.30	44.65	47.00	49.35
4.8	31.20	33.60	36.00	38.40	40.80	43.20	45.60	48.00	50.40
4.9	31.85	34.30	36.75	39.20	41.65	44.10	46.55	49.00	51.45
5.0	32.50	35.00	37.50	40.00	42.50	45.00	47.50	50.00	52.50
5.1	33.15	35.70	38.25	40.80	43.35	45.90	48.45	51.00	53.55
5.2	33.80	36.40	39.00	41.60	44.20	46.80	49.40	52.00	54.60
5.3	34.45	37.10	39.75	42.40	45.05	47.70	50.35	53.00	55.65
5.4	35.10	37.80	40.50	43.20	45.90	48.60	51.30	54.00	56.70
5.5	35.75	38.50	41.25	44.00	46.75	49.50	52.25	55.00	57.75
5.6	36.40	39.20	42.00	44.80	47.60	50.40	53.20	56.00	58.80
5.7	37.05	39.90	42.75	45.60	48.45	51.30	54.15	57.00	59.85
5.8	37.70	40.60	43.50	46.40	49.30	52.20	55.10	58.00	60.90
5.9	38.35	41.30	44.25	47.20	50.15	53.10	56.05	59.00	61.95
6.0	39.00	42.00	45.00	48.00	51.00	54.00	57.00	60.00	63.00
6.1	39.65	42.70	45.75	48.80	51.85	54.90	57.95	61.00	64.05
6.2	32.30	43.40	46.50	49.60	52.70	55.80	58.90	62.00	64.10
6.3	40.95	44.10	47.25	50.40	53.55	56.70	59.85	63.00	66.15

Hours @	$6.50	7.00	7.50	8.00	8.50	9.00	9.50	10.00	10.50
6.4	41.60	44.80	48.00	51.20	54.40	57.60	60.80	64.00	67.20
6.5	42.25	45.50	48.75	52.00	55.25	58.50	61.75	65.00	68.25
6.6	42.90	46.20	49.50	52.80	56.10	59.40	62.70	66.00	69.30
6.7	43.55	46.90	50.25	53.60	56.95	60.30	63.65	67.00	70.35
6.8	44.20	47.60	51.00	54.40	57.80	61.20	64.60	68.00	71.40
6.9	44.85	48.30	51.75	55.20	58.65	62.10	65.55	69.00	72.45
7.0	45.50	49.00	52.50	56.00	59.50	63.00	66.50	70.00	73.50
7.1	46.15	49.70	53.25	56.80	60.35	63.90	67.45	71.00	74.55
7.2	46.80	50.40	54.00	57.60	61.20	64.80	68.40	72.00	75.60
7.3	47.45	51.10	54.75	58.40	62.05	65.70	69.35	73.00	76.65
7.4	48.10	51.80	55.50	59.20	62.90	66.60	70.30	74.00	77.70
7.5	48.75	52.50	56.25	60.00	63.75	67.50	71.25	75.00	78.75
7.6	49.40	53.20	57.00	60.80	64.60	68.40	72.20	76.00	79.80
7.7	50.05	53.90	57.75	61.60	65.45	69.30	73.15	77.00	80.85
7.8	50.70	54.60	58.50	62.40	66.30	70.20	74.10	78.00	81.90
7.9	51.35	55.30	59.25	63.20	67.15	71.10	75.05	79.00	82.95
8.0	52.00	56.00	60.00	64.00	68.00	72.00	76.00	80.00	84.00
8.1	52.65	56.70	60.75	64.80	68.85	72.90	76.95	81.00	85.05
8.2	53.30	57.40	61.50	65.60	69.70	73.80	77.90	82.00	86.10
8.3	53.95	58.10	62.25	66.40	70.55	74.70	78.85	83.00	87.15
8.4	54.60	58.80	63.00	67.20	71.40	75.60	79.80	84.00	88.20
8.5	55.25	59.50	63.75	68.00	72.25	76.50	80.75	85.00	89.25
8.6	55.90	60.20	64.50	68.80	73.10	77.40	81.70	86.00	90.30
8.7	56.55	60.90	65.25	69.60	73.95	78.30	82.65	87.00	91.35
8.8	57.20	61.60	66.00	70.40	74.80	79.20	83.60	88.00	92.40
8.9	57.85	62.30	66.75	71.20	75.65	80.10	84.55	89.00	93.45
9.0	58.50	63.00	67.50	72.00	76.50	81.00	85.50	90.00	94.50
9.1	59.15	63.70	68.25	72.80	77.35	81.90	86.45	91.00	95.55
9.2	59.80	64.40	69.00	73.60	78.20	82.80	87.40	92.00	96.60
9.3	60.45	65.10	69.75	74.40	79.05	83.70	88.35	93.00	97.65
9.4	61.10	65.80	70.50	75.20	79.90	84.60	89.30	94.00	98.70
9.5	61.75	66.50	71.25	76.00	80.75	85.50	90.25	95.00	99.75
9.6	62.40	67.20	72.00	76.80	81.60	86.40	91.20	96.00	100.80
9.7	63.05	67.90	72.75	77.60	82.45	87.30	92.15	97.00	101.85
9.8	63.70	68.60	73.50	78.40	83.70	88.20	93.10	98.00	102.90
9.9	64.35	69.30	74.25	79.20	84.15	89.10	94.05	99.00	103.95
10.0	65.00	70.00	75.00	80.00	85.00	90.00	95.00	100.00	105.00

A GLOSSARY OF AUTOMOTIVE PARTS, TERMS, AND JARGON

Accelerator. The foot pedal on the extreme right in most automobiles which, when depressed, opens the throttle valve on the carburetor and allows an increased amount of fuel vapor to enter the engine's cylinders.

Acetylene. A colorless gas, C_2H_2, which when mixed with oxygen, is used for welding metals. In most garages, you will find a portable rack on wheels containing two cylinders, one containing acetylene and the other oxygen.

Acrylic Resin Paints. Almost all new cars are finished at the factory with this type of paint, and then baked at extremely high temperatures. The resulting surface is so hard that little or no polishing should be required for the first two years. Slight paint imperfections should be ignored as rubbing down prior to "fogging" the fault, breaks through the baked finish and might result after a few months in a "patchy" appearance.

Additives. Many garages make an extra profit out of an oil change by charging the customer for a quart of oil additive. Provided that the factory recommended grade of high quality oil is used, there is some question about the efficacy of this practice. It is also possible that this charge may be added to the customer's bill without the additive being used; it would be next to impossible for the customer to verify if the additive had actually been administered.

Alternator. This device has been used in place of the old-styled generator on most new cars for the past few years. The important advantage it has over the generator, provided the car battery is healthy, is that it will not lose or discharge its power no matter how much of the car's electrical equipment is being used at the same time, if the engine is turning over. The disadvantage is that it will not recharge the battery. If headlights, radio, or other power equipment are used when the engine is turned off, the battery will soon require recharging, as this lost power will not be replaced by the alternator.

Ammeter. While most cars now have only "idiot lights" in the dash which are meant to light up when there is insufficient oil pressure or a discharge of current from the battery, new car buyers can still pay a little extra and order their cars built with an oil pressure gauge and an AMMETER gauge. An AMMETER is an instrument which measures the amount of electricity in amperes being charged into or discharged from your car's battery.

Ampere. A measured unit of electricity, based on the amount of electrical current sent by one volt through a basic resistance unit called an ohm.

Antifreeze. This can be almost any liquid which has a lower freezing point than water, such as alcohol or glycerine. When added to the water in an automobile's cooling system, it gives reliable protection from corrosive rust and prevents the water from freezing to a solid block whenever air temperatures drop to and below the 32° Fahrenheit freezing point.

Anti-Knock. This describes any of the substances that can be added to the fuel of an internal combustion engine to eliminate or reduce the noise caused by combustion ignition which comes a little too early or a little too late.

Armature. An iron core wound with wire. The part of an automobile generator or electric motor which revolves.

Asbestos. A fire-resistant and heat-resistant material, which sometimes comes woven like a textile or in sheets, something like cardboard. It is used to insulate hot running machinery and to protect both humans and inflammable materials from anything which gives off a hot spark or flame.

Axle. The rod or shaft on which the wheels of an automobile revolve.

Bald. An expression used around garages to describe worn-out or smooth tires.

Ball Bearing. A bearing which uses freely rolling metal balls to carry the weight and torque of a revolving shaft.

Bevel Gear. This is a gear wheel which allows one shaft to take its drive from another running at a different angle.

Bleed the brakes. This is an expression used to describe ridding the hydraulic brake system of excess air.

Block. The body of the engine. A casting, in and around which the engine is built.

Blow-By. The first sign of a worn-out engine. If when the hood is raised and the oil filler cap is removed, oily smoke appears when the engine is running, this is called "blow-by." In almost every instance, this is a sure sign that the engine needs new piston rings.

Blow Out. In garage jargon, this does *not* mean a hearty meal. It means the bursting of a tire while a vehicle is in motion.

Bore. Your car engine probably has four, six, or eight cylinders. These are holes *bored* into the engine block in which the pistons drive the crankshaft. The size of the *bore*, or in simple terms, the diameter of the holes, is called the bore.

Brake. That which stops or slows a moving vehicle or machine, by pressing a block against a moving part.

Brake Shoe. Set just behind your car's wheels at the end of each axle are the brake drums. In simple terms, these are like flat round boxes, inside which are two semi-circular metal blocks covered with a heat resistant fibrous material. The metal blocks are called BRAKE SHOES and the fibrous covers are better known as brake linings. When you activate your brakes by pressing on the brake pedal, a hydraulic system goes into action and pushes the rounded BRAKE SHOES against the rounded inside of the round boxes, or brake drums, thus slowing or stopping the wheels and bringing the vehicle eventually to a halt.

Bushing. A removable and therefore replaceable metal lining, usually made of a softer metal than that which it supports, thus reducing friction on moving parts.

Blower. When your mechanic talks about your heater, he is referring to the fan which forces the hot air into the car. In some areas, a BLOWER is the name given to any kind of supercharger that is attached to the engine.

Bezel. You have lots of BEZELS on your car, from air conditioning control BEZELS, back-up lamp BEZELS, gas tank filler BEZELS, instrument BEZELS and lots more. A BEZEL is the rim or setting that surrounds and holds something in a decorative fashion.

Cam. A CAM is a projection on a shaft or wheel which imparts an eccentric, alternating, or otherwise irregular motion to the driving axle of a car. Possibly the most vital part of your car's engine is the camshaft, which is the digestive system which metabolises the driving power from the pistons and cylinders and transmits it all, through the transmission, to the differential gear on the driving axle.

Cant. When a mechanic talks about adjusting the CANT of a wheel or a gear, he means the tilt or slanted angle at which the wheel or gear runs most efficiently.

Car. If you don't know what this is, and you purchased this book, the author and the publisher send you their warmest regards.

Carborundum. An extremely hard abrasive substance in common use in garages and manufactured from carbons and silicones.

Carburetor. A mixing and atomizing device found on all cars with internal combustion engines. It mixes in the correct proportions (something like fifteen parts of air to one part of gasoline vapor) the explosive gas which is sprayed into the engine's combustion chambers.

Charge. When the mechanic tells you he's going to CHARGE your battery, you don't have to reach for your checkbook. He is just telling you that the supply of electricity stored in your car's battery has run down and he is going to refurbish it by connecting it for a while to a battery charger.

Chassis. The lower frame, wheels, engine, transmission, axles and differential of a motor vehicle.

Choke. This is just a small valve attached to the engine's carburetor which lowers or cuts off the supply of air to the gasoline vapor, thus making the mixture richer.

Clutch. Most of you probably know what a CLUTCH does on a car, it's time all of you knew what it is. When your car's engine is running and the transmission is in the neutral position, the car can stand quite still because the engine's power is not being transferred to the wheels by the transmission. Many of today's automobiles weigh as much as two tons and if the transmission gears were abruptly slammed against the engine's driving gears, the gear's teeth would be stripped off, or if they weren't, a drive shaft would undoubtedly break. The CLUTCH is a device which allows the stationary transmission sprocket to be gradually introduced to the great force of power coming from the engine's drive gears. It permits the transmission to pick up the engine's power output slowly by slipping until the receptive transmission gear is running at the same speed as the engine's drive gear.

Condenser. A condenser is a device for receiving and holding or storing a charge of electricity. On your automobile, the condenser can be found sitting on top of the distributor if you lift off the distributor cap. Electricity is fed into the condenser and distributed in the correct amounts to the spark plugs as each of the points make contact with its fingers. In appearance, it looks something like a small cotton reel and measures about a half inch in diameter by three-quarters of an inch long.

Core. In garage parlance, when a mechanic talks about removing a heater CORE, a radiator CORE, or any other kind of core, he is referring to the innards, or that which functions inside some kind of outer casing.

Cotter Pin. A wedge type pin or bolt that is used to hold machinery together. It is made in the form of a split pin so that after insertion, the ends may be split or spread to keep it in place.

Counter Shaft. This is any shaft which takes its drive from the main driving shaft and transmits motion to a working part.

Countersink. Simply stated, this is enlarging the top part of a screw hole so that the screw or bolt will not protrude above the surface into which the screw or bolt is driven.

Coupling. When a mechanic talks about a COUPLING, he could be referring to any device used to join moving parts together.

Cowl. Most of you have probably referred to this part of your car as the "thing-a-ma-jig" until now. The COWL is that metal housing which supports the rear of the hood, the windshield, the instrument panel and the foot pedals.

Crankcase. The metal casing in which your engine's crankshaft is housed.

Crank. Arms or levers used for imparting either rotary or oscillating motion to a rotating shaft.

Crankshaft. The main engine shaft into which are built the cranks which receive the power generated from the pistons by means of connecting rods.

Cubic Measure. Your engine will be described as being of a certain number of cubic inches in capacity. This number is not related to the horsepower of the engine directly, as many people are led to believe by the startling claims in the auto maker's advertising. It is the total number of cubic inches contained in one of your engine's cylinders, multiplied by the number of cylinders. Thus, if you have a 320 cubic inch engine that has eight cylinders, each cylinder measures 40 cubic inches. Numbers have always been deceiving of course, and to give you an idea of how deceiving they are when it comes to automobile engines, there are 1,728 cubic inches in one cubic foot, which means that the cubic capacity of five good sized car engines amounts to less than one cubic foot. Horsepower is something else of course and you can find out about that under H.

Clevis. These are used in several places around your car. It is just a useful U-shaped yoke at the end of a rod or chain, between the ends of which a lever or hook can be pinned or bolted.

Cylinder. Lots of CYLINDERS on your car, but none so important as your brake system's master CYLINDER. Many recent model cars have a double master CYLINDER arrangement and two independent brake systems and it's high time that all cars were given this minimum safety standard. Have the fluid level checked at least once every month, it could save your life and the gas station attendant is quite capable of handling this for you.

Diameter. A straight line drawn between the two furthest points of anything which is perfectly round. The measured length of this line, multiplied three and one seventh times, will give the exact measurement of the circumference or outline of the same circle.

Differential Gear. Your car's engine is probably at the front of your car. It sends its power through the transmission through a revolving shaft which passes under where you sit to the rear axle. This driving power is transferred to the rear axle with what is called the DIFFERENTIAL GEAR. In more technical terms, a DIFFERENTIAL GEAR is an epicyclic train of gears designed to permit two or more shafts to revolve at different speeds. In your car, this allows one of your rear wheels to be driven faster than the other when the car is making a turn. If the mechanic talks of your ring gear, drive shaft gear or pinion gear, these are all parts of the DIFFERENTIAL GEAR.

Disc Brakes. Probably the most efficient type of brakes ever devised. They consist of large metal discs mounted on the axles just inside each wheel. The brake is activated when these discs are squeezed between small fibrous shoes.

Distributor. Your car's engine has either four, six, or eight cylinders, each requiring combustion at a different time and in a definite sequence. The small condenser on top of the DISTRIBUTOR collects and stores the correct amount of electrical current and distributes these amounts evenly through the rotary arm and the points to the spark plug at the top of each combustion chamber.

Dynamometer. This word is now in common use around garages. It is somewhat overused to impress the more gullible service customers. A DYNAMOMETER is an electrical device which measures the output or driving torque of a rotating machine. The type generally used in garages assists the tune-up mechanic by allowing him to quickly isolate a plug, points, or coil that is causing a loss of power. It is my opinion that its greatest value to the garage owner is the effect its name has on uninformed service customers.

Dowel. When two pieces of equipment are fitted together or aligned together and subjected to vibration or stress, a DOWEL is often driven through aligned holes in both pieces to keep them rigidly in line. The best description is that a DOWEL is a kind of pin.

Duct. Your car might have an air flow DUCT, a muffler tail pipe DUCT, a defroster DUCT and an air cleaner DUCT. A DUCT is any tube, canal, pipe, or conduit by which a fluid, air, or other substance is conducted or conveyed.

Ethyl Gasoline. Contains tetraethyl lead, a poisonous lead compound added to gasoline to prevent knock in higher compression engines. Thousands of tons of this poison are pumped into the atmosphere from automobile exhausts every single day. In this writer's opinion, harmful smog would be reduced immediately by at least 80% if a law were passed banning the sale of leaded gasoline.

Escutcheon. An ornamental or protective plate around a door handle, light switch or dash instruments.

Elements. When the mechanic talks about an air cleaner ELEMENT, an oil filter ELEMENT, a gas filter ELEMENT or a cigarette lighter ELEMENT, he is refering to the heart of the unit, or the part that does the work.

Experience. This word will almost certainly be part of the sign over the garage door. It might also mention FACTORY TRAINED MECHANICS, or if they are really anxious to impress you, perhaps EXPERIENCED FACTORY TRAINED MECHANICS. They say many other things that aren't always true also.

Fan. Almost all American made car engines are water cooled. Before the water is sent into the cooling system to do its job, it is cleverly spread out thinly in the radiator (under R) while a high speed fan which takes its drive from the engine, cools it to a temperature that will keep the engine running efficiently.

Fender. Since this word was first used to describe a section of an automobile, both the shapes of the cars and the meaning of the word FENDER have changed somewhat. Nowadays, a FENDER would seem to be any part of the side body in front of the doors or behind the doors. Originally, it described the curved section of metal which covered each of the wheels, or what we now call the wheel arches.

Fiberglas. This is a textile made by weaving very finely spun filaments of glass. The new FIBERGLAS tires have a belt of this material running all around the tire. As this material is extremely strong and resists heat expansion, it ensures far greater stability and longer life to automobile tires.

Fog. This is garage jargon and describes using a paint spray gun with a very light and skillful touch to correct a small paint fault. To "fog in the paint," or "fogging the paint."

Freezing Point. When the temperature drops down to around 32° Fahrenheit or 0° Centigrade, you'd better have something more than water in your car's radiator. At these temperatures, water by itself will freeze to a solid block of ice. Water expands considerably when it freezes and if this is allowed to take place in your car's cooling system, things will be "busting out all over" and your repair bill could be astronomical. There are many excellent antifreeze additives available at your garage and I recommend that you use one of them at all times, even when the weather is fine. They do more than lower considerably the freezing point in your car's cooling system. At the other extreme, they help to prevent overheating as well, as they stabilize the temperature of all the liquid in your car's cooling system.

Friction. The resistance to motion of surfaces that touch.

Flange. A FLANGE is used to give added strength to a metal fitting. It is a projecting rim, collar or rim on a shaft, pipe, machine housing that is formed to give additional strength.

Gasket. Because a perfectly flat surface is almost an impossibility, when two flat metal surfaces are bolted together and subjected to either internal or external pressure, gases, water or oil are going to find their way between the two joined surfaces. Therefore, to prevent messy leaks and loss of pressure, a softer material of the same size and shape as the two metal surfaces to be joined is placed between them so that as they are tightened together, any miniscule imperfections on the two metal surfaces are sealed into the softer shaped seal. It is this softer shaped seal that is called a GASKET.

Gears. These are wheels with teeth shaped into the outer edges, so that the motion of one is passed on to the others.

Generator. Simply stated, this is a machine which receives mechanical energy from an outside source and transforms it into electrical energy.

Governor. This is a mechanical contraption which automatically controls the top speed of a car or truck by regulating the intake of fuel at the carburetor.

Grape. You know a GRAPE as a fruit that is easily digested and one which could be quite easily peeled. Automobile dealerships and garages use the word GRAPE to describe to each other a customer who is easy to handle, easy to swindle and easy to sell.

Horsepower. This is kind of difficult to explain in simple terms. It's important however that you realize that it does not always follow that the more horsepower your car has, the faster it will go. Some of the fastest cars in the world have quite small engines with relatively low horsepower ratings. The Aston Martin for instance, was tested recently by an authoritative American publication. From a standing start, it went to 100 miles per hour and was brought to a stop in just 26 seconds. Try and equal that in your high horsepowered family car. If we had a little less horsepower around and a little more quality engineering, we'd most assuredly have a lot less smog. What is horsepower? If you must know, it's a foot-pound-second unit of power, equivalent to 550 foot-pounds per second

Hydrometer. An instrument used for measuring the specific gravity of liquids.

Hydraulic. Machinery that is operated by the applied pressure of a liquid, as in HYDRAULIC brakes.

Ignition. On your car, the IGNITION system is the intricate series of electrical devices that collect, store, and distribute the correct amount of current to IGNITE the spark plug which, in turn, IGNITES the explosive mixture in each cylinder.

Journeyman. Not too many years ago, this was the proud title given to a man who had qualified for his trade after serving his apprenticeship. Nowadays, it doesn't mean much of anything, as the idea of a young man spending five years learning how to be a highly skilled automotive engineer seems to be something to be scoffed at. After all, it really doesn't require very much training to throw away a perfectly good set of spark plugs and install a new set, right?

Lag Bolt. A bolt with a square head.

Linch-Pin. The name given to the pin that goes through the end of an axle outside the wheel to keep the wheel from coming off. I'm quite sure that the wheels on today's automobiles are kept on more securely than that. LINCH-PINS are used on smaller wheels and smaller axles in all kinds of machinery.

Manifold. If you examine the side of your engine block, you will find a good sized pipe with either four or six shorter pipes coming from the side of the engine and branching into it. This is called the exhaust MANIFOLD and it is through this apparatus that the exhaust fumes leave the cylinders and are conducted to the exhaust pipes and out into the atmosphere where they are almost immediately recognizable as smog.

Mechanic. Anyone who wants to call himself one. I guess the true definition today would be anyone who can persuade a shorthanded garage owner to employ him as one. Most other trades and professions are controlled by a governing body of their contemporaries and are required to prove that they have absorbed a certain number of years of training and to demonstrate their skills during a difficult trade test. In far too many states in this country, no trade test is required and no license is even available.

Miss. When one or more of the spark plugs in your car fails to ignite the explosive vapor in its combustion chamber, this is called a MISS in the garage business.

Muffler. This means exactly what it says. It's a metal box which muffles or silences the roaring sound of the exhaust gasses as they are exploded out of the combustion chambers. You'll find it somewhere underneath the rear part of your car, usually between and just behind the rear wheels. It's quite a simple arrangement really. The noisy exhaust is fed in at one end of the muffler box which is packed with deadening materials like asbestos and fiberglas. The smog is then quietly pumped into our environment through the short tailpipe at the other end of the MUFFLER box.

Octane. You probably don't know what OCTANE really means, although you are quite sure that it has something to do with the power in gasoline. Gasolines all seem to have a number known as the OCTANE rating. The higher the OCTANE rating number, the more powerful the gasoline, right? Wrong! Here briefly, is a simple definition of OCTANE. It is an oily hydrocarbon of the paraffin family, added to almost all gasolines to cut down the ping or knock problem that occurs with high compression engines. The OCTANE rating is simply a number given to denote the antiknock quality of a gasoline. The higher the number, the greater this quality.

Piston. Your car has the same number of PISTONS as it has cylinders. A PISTON is a short cylinder fitted inside a hollow cylinder. It is moved up and down the hollow cylinder by the pressure caused by gasoline and air vapors exploding in the combustion chamber. Its motion is transmitted to a piston rod, in some parts called a connecting rod. The PISTON and the connecting rod are held together by a piston pin or a wrist pin. This permits the rectilinear motion of the PISTON to become rotary motion when the connecting rod is joined to the crankshaft.

Piston Ring. On each of the pistons mentioned above, PISTON RINGS or packing rings are fitted into small grooves. These are split and therefore expandable so as to ensure that the pistons fit tightly against the walls of the cylinders.

Points. The points can be found underneath the distributor cap on your car. It's just a pair of contacts that look something like a small pair of tweezers similar to the kind you use to remove a splinter from your finger. The POINTS of these contacts are usually tipped with either platinum or tungsten.

Polarity. Don't worry too much about the word, but I must warn you to be very careful when you're poking around under the hood of your car with a screwdriver or anything made of metal in your hand. You see, the POLARITY of any electrical circuit is the condition of having magnetic poles (one positive and one negative). The circuit between your battery and your generator or alternator must remain polarized at all times if the electricity drawn from your battery is to be replaced. One very frequent and profitable task that service garages are called upon to perform is caused by overzealous amateur mechanics who thrive on poking around under the hood of their car. The vulnerable spot is the voltage regulator. This is usually attached to either the engine cowl or just inside the front fender, in the engine compartment. It always has a plastic cover and measures about four or five inches square. A heavy grade of insulated copper wires run into this box at the side and sometimes the insulation becomes ineffective due to oil vapor and heat. A carelessly handled screwdriver in the area of the voltage regulator would immediately *reverse the polarity* of the circuit between the generator and the battery, thus causing the electrical charge to drawn out of the battery instead of the steady charge being fed into it. This would ultimately ruin the battery and certainly bring your car to a stop before too many miles. A crooked garage could easily sell you a new generator, a new battery, and a new voltage regulator if you don't know about POLARITY.

Rack and Pinion Steering. In this context, a RACK is a straight bar with teeth cut into one of its sides, adapted to engage with a PINION, so as to convert the circular motion of the PINION into the rectilinear motion of the RACK. You turn your steering wheel in a circular motion, at the other end of the steering column is the PINION, with its teeth engaged in the RACK. The turning PINION moves the rack back and forth, thus turning the front axle and wheels and allowing you to control the direction your car takes.

Radiator. On all water-cooled automobile engines, the radiator is situated at very front of the engine compartment, with one side facing the engine and the other side facing the cold onrushing air as your car moves along. On the engine side, a good sized cooling fan also helps to cool down the RADIATOR. It's really a very simple way of receiving the very hot water that has picked up the heat while circulating the engine, quickly spreading it out in the RADIATOR shell, cooling it down with the outside onrushing air and the inside fan, and then sending it back through the cooling system again to maintain a workable engine temperature.

Shock Absorber. These words explain themselves, so don't be scared of them. SHOCK ABSORBERS are simply mechanical devices attached underneath your car close to each corner. There are several different types in common use, but all of them serve the same purpose. The springs on your car permits the vehicle to run over deep pot-holes and bumps in the road without your being given a severe jar. As the spring goes down and gives you a comfortable ride, naturally it must continue to go up and down until the springing motion has subsided. You can imagine what that would be like. Every time your car goes over a bump, you would continue to go up and down for half a block. Here is where your SHOCK ABSORBERS do their job. They have nothing to do with taking the *shock* out of a bump in the road, your springs do that for you. The SHOCK ABSORBERS simply absorb the upward movement of the springs, so that after going over the bump, your car only goes down once and then comes up into the tender ABSORBING arms of your SHOCK ABSORBERS.

Solenoid. What happens when you turn your key to start your car? You send electrical current from your battery to the starter switch or in mechanic's terms, the SOLENOID switch. Here, the current enters a small coil inside which is an iron core. This creates a magnet and pulls the starter motor's contacts together so that the starter motor is activated. That's my definition in words that I hope you'll understand. If you'd like the technical definition of the word SOLENOID, it's an electric conductor wound as a helix with small pitch, or as two or more coaxial helices, so that current through the conductor establishes a magnetic field within the conductor. Don't you get the impression that they really aren't anxious for you to understand?

Stroke. You will often hear the expression, "the bore and STROKE of an engine" and if you refer back under the "Bs," you'll learn again what the bore of an engine is all about. The STROKE of your engine is the exact distance one of the pistons travels during one extreme of its range to the other, either while it moves up the cylinder or while it moves down the cylinder.

Suspension. Your car's SUSPENSION is the entire system of springs and other devices which support the body of the vehicle upon its undercarriage.

Thermostat. The word therm is one of several units of heat. The thermometer in your home or office indicates the heat in the room's atmosphere. The word STAT means stationary and that should lead you easily into the meaning of the word THERMOSTAT, a device which maintains heat or temperature at the same intensity. The THERMOSTAT on your car is built into the cooling system to help stabilize the temperature of the circulating coolant. It is quite a small and inexpensive item and its replacement will often cure any overheating problems your engine might develop.

Tie Rods. The entire steering efficiency of your car depends on these small steel rods which connect your front wheels to the steering mechanism. Have them checked every time your car is in for service, especially if your steering doesn't feel right.

Torque. Here's another word in common usage around a garage. In plain language, it means the force put out by a driven turning shaft and transmitted to another mechanical device. It's a force which tends to produce a twisting or rotating motion. In technical terms, it is the measured ability of a rotating element, such as a gear or a shaft to overcome turning resistance.

Torque Converter. This is a vital part of your automatic transmission. It is a fluid coupling in which three or more rotors are used, one of which can be checked so that output TORQUE is augmented and output speed is diminished.

Torsion Bar. The word TORSION is related to the word torque, in so far as they both refer to a twisting motion. TORSION BARS are used by some car manufacturers as part of the suspension system on their vehicles. They are metal bars that have elasticity when subjected to torsion.

Transmission. On your car this is the unit which transmits the power output of your engine to the wheels in gradual and controlled amounts, using a system of gears and torque.

Un-Horse. This is an expression used by the automobile trade to describe persuading the customer to leave his car at the dealership or garage.

Universal Joint. When the mechanic has said, "You have a bad UNIVERSAL that's causing that noise under your car." Haven't you ever wondered to yourself, "What the heck is a UNIVERSAL?"

Here's the answer. The drive-shaft runs under the car from the transmission to the differential gear at the rear axle. It is broken half way there and joined by a coupling which allows the rest of the shaft to run at a slightly different angle from the first part. This special kind of coupling is called a UNIVERSAL JOINT.

There are, of course many more words and names of parts used around garages. In fact the manufacturer's parts book which just lists all of the parts stocked by a parts department, is many times the size of this whole book. So I have not included words that you will never come into contact with, neither have I attempted to explain the meaning of such words as speedometer, spark plug, tire, or wheel. These are words you can find out about at your public library for a good deal less time, effort, and money than would be required from you at the service department of your local new car agency or the branch of your neighborhood franchise dealer, and that, of course, is the idea behind this book.

OTHER TITLES IN THE SHERBOURNE PRESS HANDBOOK SERIES

ENERGETICS: YOUR KEY TO WEIGHT CONTROL

by Grant Gwinup, M.D.

Energetics is a basic system in which caloric credits are balanced against debits—there are credits for all activities, no matter how strenuous or passive (300 for an hour of slow biking, 50 for an hour of knitting, 600 for an hour of jogging)—and there are debits for all food consumed.

Medically correct charts and tables help you figure out your own debit-credit system to lose as much weight as you want and keep that weight off indefinitely.

Dr. Gwinup, a specialist in weight problems, is chairman of the division of endocrinology at the University of California (Irvine), and director of the Metabolic Research Laboratory. His book stresses how it is possible to obtain significant long-term weight loss without drugs, special devices, diuretics, steaming sessions, or machines that actually traumatize the body. In fact, Dr. Gwinup openly encourages between-meal snacks and urges the reader to eat his favorite foods.

"The one sensible way to diet." *Look Magazine*

"A fascinating new book." *Vogue Magazine*

"A remarkable book." *House Beautiful Magazine*

178 pages, charts, tables

$4.95

THE SMALL INVESTOR'S HANDBOOK FOR LONG-TERM
SECURITY OR QUICK PROFIT

by Ogden D. Scoville

By following the direct, non-speculative, no nonsense advice
in this book, the reader, regardless of his income bracket or source,
can gain a clear investment picture and learn how to put his
money to work for him.

Written by a man who advises thousands of clients every
year, this book gets down to cases immediately by helping the
reader decide what kind of investor he is, then helping him to
take the initial steps toward a long-term program, the high-
profit "flyer," or the investment fund. Detailed chapters on stocks,
bonds, and mutual funds are augmented by discussions on mis-
cellaneous investments that are making small investors richer
by the day.

Here is realistic investment for the small investor whose
modest funds can also become "smart money."

"It will help the reader . . ." *Off the Press Magazine*
156 pages
$4.95

The text for Sherbourne Press handbooks is linotype Caledonia. The titles and chapter headings are set in varying sizes of Helvetica. Paper is Sherbourne Special Book, supplied by Perkins and Squier. Cover material is Holliston Sturdetan #142 Crushed Morocco. The format for this and other Sherbourne Press Handbooks was developed by Shirley Shipley.